Career Counseling
and
Placement
in Higher Education:

A Student Personnel Function

Career Counseling
and
Placement
in Higher Education:

A Student Personnel Function

BY EVERETT W. STEPHENS

THE COLLEGE PLACEMENT COUNCIL, INC.

THE AUTHOR

EVERETT W. STEPHENS, vice president of Babson College, has spent 30 years in student personnel work, including both student counseling and teaching assignments in psychology and education at Anatolia College (Thessaloniki, Greece), Northeastern University, Boston University, and Babson College. At Babson he has held successively the posts of director of placement, dean of students, and, now that of vice president.

He served on his local school board several terms, is a past president of Eastern College Personnel Officers, past vice president for association relations of the College Placement Council, and former chairman of Commission VI (Placement) of the American College Personnel Association.

The author is also an occasional contributor to various publications, writing in the areas of placement, counseling, psychological testing and personality. In his latest writing in the *Journal of College Placement,* he co-authored articles which were the products of nationwide studies on "What Are the Attitudes of Students Toward Occupations?" (December 1966–January 1967) and "Who and What Influence Student Attitudes Toward Occupations?" (February–March 1968).

Dr. Stephens is currently a member of the corporation of the Perry School in Boston, and is chairman of the Board of Trustees of Anatolia College.

© *Copyright 1970 by*
THE COLLEGE PLACEMENT COUNCIL, INC.
65 East Elizabeth Ave., Bethlehem, Pennsylvania
Library of Congress Catalog Number 77-138318

Acknowledgments

I owe a special debt of gratitude to the discerning members of the College Placement Council Publications Sub-Committee who gave so willingly of their time to read manuscript and give me helpful criticism and intelligent direction: Drue E. Matthews, chairman; Warren E. Kauffman, Alfred R. Looman, Fannie Y. Mitchell, and Ronald R. Pariseau.

To my long-time associate, my sharpest and most helpful critic, Elizabeth C. Kebbe, I am grateful once again for astute comments.

I owe much, also, to Nancy D. Stevens, Alva C. Cooper, and Raymond H. Stockard who, more than they may realize, were most effective reactors to ideas.

For source material, my thanks to Robert Calvert, Jr., Robert F. Menke, Robert J. Morrissey, Chester C. Arnold, J. W. Souther, and James L. Galloway, and the presidents of each of the regional placement associations.

To my office staff at Babson, and especially to my secretary, Mrs. Jo-Anne Kelly, who on various occasions came to my rescue with their help, I am deeply grateful.

As great as my debt of gratitude is to the many, my deepest

appreciation is for my understanding wife, Mary, who put up with me while I hibernated night after night and weekend after weekend during winter evenings and summer holidays.

And to those of you who read the book, thanks, too. If it doesn't provoke you to react, then the book has not fully served its purpose.

Everett W. Stephens
Babson College
Wellesley, Massachusetts

Foreword

Career Counseling and Placement in Higher Education: A Student Personnel Function is, in its original intent, a revision of *The Fundamentals of College Placement,* a text on the field published first in 1962 by the College Placement Council. Actually, it is much more; it is in most ways a new presentation of the fundamentals of the field, its philosophy, principles, and rationale, its relationship with other functional areas within the educational enterprise, as well as with the "nuts and bolts" of career counseling and placement offices. The title itself reflects developments in the field and, hopefully, the increased breadth and sophistication of the college placement activity on most college and university campuses.

It has not been possible, in one volume, to do justice to any one topic. Many chapters could usefully be expanded into separate books. The effort of the writer, with the complete endorsement of his advisory committee, has been to give a valid and valuable overview of the field. Each chapter has been carefully researched, however, and anyone interested in giving himself (or others) a comprehensive course on career counseling and placement or in delving more deeply into any one of the subjects covered could do no better than to use the footnotes and the bibliography for each chapter as assigned reading.

Since the career counseling and placement field is still in its adolescence, although perhaps out of its infancy, a number of chapters are provocative rather than definitive. The intent, in these cases, has been to stimulate thinking, to encourage the imaginative response, to invite experimentation in the solution of the perennial problems which characterize any educational enterprise. Both the writer and the committee hope that much of *Career Counseling and Placement* will be read with this in mind.

In line with this spirit, there has been an attempt in several places to look ahead 10 years or so—an attempt that is always a bit dangerous and certain to be controversial. The next revision of this basic text can evaluate our effort.

Now, for those readers who may be interested in knowing more about how this particular book came about, to whom it is directed, and how it grew, some additional information is presented.

In June 1965 at the annual meeting of the College Placement Council, the Publications Committee was first charged with revising the *Fundamentals of College Placement*. This textbook on placement had been completed in 1962, the product of a massive committee project, taking several years. Although still useful, the sentiment had grown that some updating of materials was desirable.

A sub-committee of the Publications Committee was formed to oversee the revision. The committee not only reread the original quite critically, but also invited comments, criticisms, and ideas from placement and recruiting people far and wide. A number of individuals volunteered criticism, advice, and material of their own. Where used in recognizable form the latter has been acknowledged in the text, but there is no way to identify adequately and give credit for all the contributions and stimulation of the sub-committee's thinking that stemmed from this grass roots action.

The initial task of the committee was seen as a determination of the audience to which a revised text on college placement should be directed. First in importance and numbers are those who are already working in the colleges and universities—those who are doing both placement and the career counseling that is more and more seen as the basic function of the student/alumnus service. Those to whom they report—deans, college presidents, vice presidents of student affairs—were also thought of as potential readers of such a text.

Another element in the audience consisted of those persons who are entering or who are considering entrance into the field. Also included are those who are teaching counselors and/or student personnel workers.

Finally, a potential audience was seen among those who must work closely and cooperatively with career counseling and placement personnel and who therefore need to understand the basic philosophy and values in the field: those administrators in the colleges or universities, especially in other student personnel areas, whose work is parallel with and coordinate to placement; those in charge of recruiting, college relations, or personnel in business, industry, and government.

After analyzing the needs of these varied publics and critically evaluating *Fundamentals of College Placement,* the sub-committee came to two conclusions:

First, the task was seen as involving a *rewriting* rather than a *revision* of the book. The original had served its purpose well with its emphasis on "nuts and bolts," with numerous samples of forms and other how-to-do-it advice. Written as it had been, each chapter by a different committee, coherent statements about principles and philosophy were lacking. Besides, principles and philosophy had been developing with increased sophistication and substance since the early '6os. It was agreed that substantial space should be given to such considerations, while at the same time providing basic how-to-do-it sections. (The best how-to-do-it assistance is increasingly seen as stemming from actual visits to established and respected placement offices rather than from printed information. The number of these visits has of course increased dramatically since *Fundamentals* appeared.)

Second, the committee took the position that a properly

developed and coherent text of this nature was not likely to result from committee writing so it proposed to the College Placement Council that the committee be authorized to make a contract with a writer who would be given both guidelines and considerable freedom and with whom close contact would be maintained.

In 1967 both of these conclusions were endorsed at the annual meeting of the Council. Everett Stephens of Babson College agreed to undertake the writing and the implementation of the project began with a joint meeting between the members of the sub-committee and the author. Since that initial exchange of ideas, an unusually fine working relationship has been maintained, the committee reading and commenting freely on chapters as they were produced. There also were several exciting and fruitful meetings at which the final drafts were reviewed.

The project, of course, took longer than anyone expected initially due to the special assignments given to the writer by his institution and to the additional time lag that committee supervision of a project necessarily entails.

The committee takes pride and satisfaction in presenting this cooperative effort. Where Everett Stephens found time and energy for the background reading as well as for the writing we do not know, but our thanks go to his understanding wife as well as to him for a responsibility excellently discharged.

College Placement Council
Publications Sub-Committee
Miss Drue E. Matthews, Chairman
Mount Holyoke College
Alfred R. Looman
Valparaiso University
Miss Fannie Y. Mitchell
Duke University
Ronald R. Pariseau
John Hancock Mutual Life Insurance Company
Warren E. Kauffman
College Placement Council

Table of Contents

xi

CHAPTER 4
Placement Office Services

CHAPTER 5
Organization and Facility Patterns

CHAPTER 6
Occupational Information and Vocational Library

CHAPTER 7
Psychological Testing and Counseling

CHAPTER 8
Automation in Placement

CHAPTER 9
The Problems of Effective Communication

CHAPTER 10
Some Legal and Ethical Aspects of Student Personnel Work

CHAPTER 11
Special Challenges to Counselors

CHAPTER 12
The Junior College and Placement

CHAPTER 13
The Campus Interview—A Vital Learning Experience for Student and Employer

CHAPTER 14
Professional Associations

CHAPTER 15
Outlook for Career Counseling and Placement

A Word About Terminology

GUIDANCE HAS BEEN defined in various ways: as self-analysis and self-direction; [1] as education; [2, 3, 4] as assistance in making choices; [5, 6] and in recent years as a clinical process of analysis, synthesis, diagnosis, prognosis, counseling, and follow-up. Because guidance as an organized discipline has carried a vocational connotation from its beginnings in the National Vocational Guidance Association, there has been widespread acceptance of the NVGA definition of vocational guidance: "the process of assisting the individual to choose an occupation, to prepare for, to enter upon, and to progress in it." [7] Guidance, then, is an all-inclusive process of motivating the best development of the individual.

Unhappily, because of abuse, the term "guidance" has fallen into disrepute with some professionals. Anna Reed, for example, rejected the term as long ago as the mid-'30s because guidance had become "a commercialized racket." [8] Other professionals, among them Williamson, Darley, and Wiener, have discarded the term "guidance" because it has been confused with advising or because it is Pollyannish on the one hand and paternalistic on the other. They prefer the term "counseling."

1

This term tends to be used loosely, and there are those who use "counseling" when they really mean "advising." Advising is the giving of information and advice; this is not counseling. A good amount of advising goes on in every placement office.

Froehlich says: "There is only one kind of counseling. Its objective is to assist individuals in making choices which lead to lives that are individually satisfying and socially effective." [9] Froehlich, on the basis of this definition, says that counseling is a process by which an individual is stimulated to (1) evaluate himself and his opportunities; (2) make a feasible choice in the light of his unique characteristics and opportunities; (3) accept responsibility for his choice; (4) initiate a course of action consonant with his choice . . ." [9]

Froehlich further differentiates between teaching, counseling, and psychotherapy: ". . . teaching is the process of providing learning experiences in line with a student's needs . . . counseling stimulates the individual to evaluate, make, accept, and act upon his choices . . . psychotherapy is the treatment of illness . . . it demands that . . . somebody be sick." [9]

Until Carl Rogers' publication, *Counseling and Psychotherapy*, in 1942 [10] counseling was considered synonymous with guidance. Since Rogers' publication, there has been a differentiation of function between guidance and counseling. Guidance, the psychologist argues, is distributive; counseling is adjustive.[11] Guidance must always follow counseling, never precede. Counseling is concerned with the organization and adjustment of the total personality; it is a process of self-evaluation. Guidance begins where counseling leaves off; it motivates the student to acquire information about the world of work and search out occupations compatible with the self-evaluation that may lead to self-fulfillment.

Some readers may believe that this controversy over definition is little more than a battle of semantics. They are probably in good company for there are those who believe the debate over definition is a classical example of what happens when overspecialized professionals become more concerned with their special skills and techniques than they are with their reason for being: to aid students in making the best use of their potential.

However, the controversy serves one worthwhile purpose; it points up the fact that placement educators, if they are both to counsel and guide, need a broad understanding of the fields of psychology. The controversy should also give pause to the logic in recent placement office name changes. Certainly "bureau of appointments" is both restrictive and non-guidance flavored; but the name "Office of Career Counseling" in the light of current definition implies considerable psychologically oriented counseling along with vocational guidance. Many placement offices are really vocational guidance centers, prepared to take up where the counseling service leaves off.

And what about the term "placement?" This term is vague, misleading, and restrictive. It implies placement in a job. Placement today, in the sophisticated office, is far more than connecting individuals with jobs. Placement is a means of helping students understand themselves through counseling, of aiding in the clarification of life goals and educational and job objectives through guidance, and of advising and helping to make education and employer contacts. It is in this sense that the term "placement" is used throughout the pages that follow.

BIBLIOGRAPHY

1 Parsons, Frank, *Choosing a Vocation,* Houghton Mifflin Co., Boston, 1909, pp. 4–5.

2 Hawkes, H. E., and A. L. R., *Through a Dean's Open Door,* McGraw-Hill Book Co., N.Y., 1945, p. 37.

3 Keller, Franklin J., "Same Door Wherein I Went: A Confession of Faith in Guidance as Education," *Occupations,* May 1935, pp. 689 ff.

4 Hildreth, Gertrude H., "Guidance in the Lincoln School," *Teachers College Record,* February 1936, p. 432.

5 Jones, Arthur J., *Principles of Guidance,* McGraw-Hill Book Co., N.Y., 1951, pp. 78 ff.

6 Myers, George E., *Principles and Techniques of Vocational Guidance,* McGraw-Hill Book Co., N.Y., 1941, pp. 15 ff.

7 NVGA position statement on "The Principles and Practices of Educational and Vocational Guidance," *Occupations,* May 1937, pp. 772 ff.

8 Reed, Anna Y. "Is Guidance a Racket?" *N.E.A. Proceedings,* June 1938, p. 628.

[9] Froehlich, Clifford P., "Counseling, Its Use and Abuse," part of a collection of readings found in "Guidance Readings for Counselors," Rand McNally & Co., Chicago (Farwell & Peters), 1959, pp. 369 ff.

[10] Rogers, Carl R., *Counseling and Psychotherapy*, Houghton Mifflin Co., Boston, 1942.

[11] Butler, John M., "On the Role of Directive and Non-directive Techniques in the Counseling Process," *Educational and Psychological Measurement*, Summer 1948, p. 208.

CHAPTER 1

Changing Perspectives in Counseling and Placement

H ERACLITUS WAS RIGHT; there is nothing more permanent than change. Higher education today is caught up in the turbulence of revolution in subject matter, teaching methods, and student values and behavior. Student activists have forced the doors to the ivory tower wide open. Student personnel work in a restless student society imposes certain conditions for success—a flexibility of personality and a dynamic philosophy of counseling, guidance, and placement.

The placement director, on occasion, has been criticized as philosophically shallow and lacking in adequate educational preparation. And it has been alleged by some that career counseling and placement operate without any proven set of hypotheses. While this may be so in some instances, there are many placement directors who have offered outstanding leadership in both philosophy and practice, particularly since World War II.

There is utilitarian value in examining the past. By so doing, the student personnel worker can see how the social, economic, educational, and intellectual temper of the times conditioned the development of the profession. Furthermore, a look at where the profession has been and where it is now enables the student personnel worker to understand how he can help to make it better in the future.

Counseling—the Saving of Souls

The counseling of students in American colleges, until well into the late 1800s and early 1900s, rested, for the most part, in the hands of the college president who, in those days, was all things to all people. Many college presidents were clergymen, more interested in saving souls than developing intellects or preparing young people for employment. There was "a persistent emphasis on extracurricular religion, and also a considerable snooping into the personal lives of the students." [1] To give the reader some idea of the degree of concern over soul-saving, Yale had 16 compulsory chapels per week, including 4 on Sunday. In addition, there were 4 voluntary noon prayer meetings each week plus frequent revival meetings. Of Amherst, at the turn of the century, it was said that "no class has ever left Amherst College without witnessing a powerful revival in religion." [2]

Interest in Students as Individuals

The passage of the Land Grant College Act in 1862 established new utilitarian types of colleges, and in the early 1900s lay presidents began to increase greatly in number. It is reputed that President Gilman of Johns Hopkins University appointed the first so-called "chief of faculty advisors" in 1899, stating that "in every institution there should be one or more persons specifically appointed to be counselors or advisors of students." [2]

In the record, there is a prophetic lecture delivered in 1899 by Dr. W. R. Harper of Chicago. This unusual address, "The

Scientific Study of the Student," was delivered at Brown University. The gist of that speech follows:

> ". . . in order that the student may receive the assistance so essential to his highest success, another step in the onward evolution will take place. This step will be the scientific study of the student himself . . . In the time that is coming, provision must be made, either by the regular instructors, or by those appointed especially for the purpose, to study in detail the man or woman to whom instruction is offered.
>
> "This (study) will be made (1) with special reference to his character . . . to find out whether he is responsible or careless, shiftless, or perhaps vicious; (2) with special reference likewise to his intellectual capacity; (3) with reference to his special intellectual characteristics to learn whether he is independent or original; (4) with reference to his special capacities and tastes; (5) with reference to the social side of his nature.
>
> "This feature of Twentieth Century education will come to be regarded as of greatest importance, and fifty years hence will prevail as widely as it is now lacking." [3]

Meanwhile, interest in individuals, for reasons other than soul saving, began to get the attention of prominent educators. In 1862 Charles W. Eliot, president of Harvard University, speaking before the National Education Association at Saratoga, New York, had this to say:

> "Democratic society does not undertake to fly in the face of nature by asserting that all children are . . . alike and should be treated alike . . . Every child is a unique personality . . . It is for the interest of society . . . that every individual

child's peculiar gifts and powers should be developed and trained to the highest degree . . ." [4]

Wilhelm Wundt, in the world's first psychological laboratory started in Germany in 1879, established the hypothesis that human behavior conforms to certain natural law and hence can be scientifically investigated. Investigations of behavior by Galton in London and Hall in America followed closely upon Wundt's pronouncement. In 1898, Jesse B. Davis, in later years the dean of the School of Education at Boston University, became the first vocational guidance counselor working with students at Central High School in Detroit.

Some years later (1902) John Dewey was beginning to develop his philosophy of education which ultimately altered the course of all education. In a publication titled *The Child and The Curriculum,* Dewey maintained that "personality and character is more than subject matter," and that as educators "we must take our stand with the child . . ." for ". . . it is he and not subject matter which determines quality and quantity of learning . . ." [5]

The Dewey philosophy pointed up the need for individual counseling and at the same time encouraged a kind of popular notion that once a student was admitted to college, it was the responsibility of that college to help the student succeed. Student failure in the early decades of the Twentieth Century was laid at the door of the college, not the student.

The first formal curriculum in college student personnel education was taught, so we are told, by Dr. Paul Monroe in the Columbia University 1916 summer session. [6]

Professional Organizations

Very early in the development of interest in students as individuals, a kind of professional fragmentation set in, with small professional groups espousing special areas of operation such as vocational guidance, college placement, student counseling, *ad infinitum.*

There came into being such professional organizations as the National Vocational Guidance Association (1913), and the National Association of Appointment Secretaries (1924)—the forerunner of the American College Personnel Association (1951). There followed numerous other professional organizations; among them were the Association for Counselor Education and Supervision, the Student Personnel Association for Teacher Education, the American School Counselor Association, the American Rehabilitation Counseling Association, the Association for Measurement and Evaluation in Guidance, and the National Employment Counselors Association.

This pattern led to petty rivalries and professional jealousies; it was not until 1952 that an umbrella organization was incorporated (the American Personnel and Guidance Association) in the hope that cooperation between the various groups could be brought about. A further attempt to coordinate organizations dealing with student personnel activities developed in 1963 with the formation of the Council of Student Personnel Associations in Higher Education.

Impact of Parsons' Theory of Vocational Choice

Vocational guidance and placement developed as one of the early, fragmented, student personnel activities. Although the National Vocational Guidance Association was formed in 1913, a Boston educator and social worker is generally credited with being the real motivator of vocational counseling and placement. Our heritage from Frank Parsons was the first theory of vocational choice which received widespread attention. In his counseling at the Vocational Bureau of Boston at the turn of the century, Parsons reasoned that young people floundered vocationally because they did not know themselves, and because they did not know how to relate themselves to jobs. Out of his experiences in counseling, Parsons developed a theory of vocational choice which he described in his book *Choosing a Vocation,* published posthumously.[7]

Every practitioner of guidance and placement should read Parsons' text. On pages 4–5, Parsons set forth his three-step theory of vocational choice:

1. self-understanding on the part of the client: a knowledge of his interests, aptitudes, resources, limitations, etc.;
2. knowledge of the world of work: aptitudes required on a job, educational background necessary, paths of advancement, remuneration, etc.;
3. matching of individual qualifications to job requirements.

This was a simple, workable hypothesis: reasoned vocational choice in the light of man-analysis and job-analysis. Parsons' book became the bible of vocational guidance for years to come. In fact, Parsons' theory of vocational choice remains the rationale of many a counselor today.

There were forces at work that contributed to the widespread acceptance of Parsons' theory. Psychological laboratories, both in Europe and America, were then probing human behavior; Binet had already commenced work in mental measurement. Following World War I, Western Electric opened the door to research into human behavior on the job; labor- and job-analysis became routine. And with concern evidenced for the abnormal personality, the mental hygiene movement was born. Increased sensitivity to the individual pointed up the need for developing techniques to deal with individual differences. World War II, the G.I. Bill, and the Veterans Administration counseling programs gave considerable impetus to the Parsons' theory. The G.I. was tested to find his interests, abilities, and personality traits. An educational program was selected which, on paper at least, would seem to fulfill best a man's test pattern (a strictly Parsonian exercise). The college placement office, in turn, made available occupational information so that, hopefully, interests, abilities, and educational background could be matched to jobs. Such a simple procedure!

Companies searching to find ways through the morass of job applications, in those post-war years, began to hire under a

Parsons' rationale: test them; match their abilities to abilities required on the job. So, vast numbers got Activity Vector Analyzed,* Wonderlicked,** and Kleinized.***

For nearly 40 years, little that was significantly new in vocational counseling appeared on the scene. In 1950, however, Dr. Eli Ginzberg, an economist at Columbia University, both annoyed and shocked guidance counselors and placement directors at the annual convention of the National Vocational Guidance Association with the statement that year after year vocational counselors and placement directors continued to counsel about vocational choice without really knowing how vocational choices are made. He chided them for their "busyness" as practitioners and their failure to be concerned professionally about research, theory, and understanding of how vocational choices are really made.

In fairness to placement directors, in the light of the Ginzberg criticism, it should be noted that college placement activities never really got into high gear until after World War II; many colleges had no placement offices until then. Those offices that were in existence pre-war were, for the most part, brokers of jobs, although there were notable exceptions. The fact remains that little of a creative nature was accomplished in placement between the two wars.

There was a tendency in many colleges to divorce counseling from placement. Student counselors, under the aegis of the National Vocational Guidance Association and the National Association of Student Personnel Administrators, developed accredited courses of study and professional standards. Placement directors, on the other hand, understaffed and besieged both by company recruiters and hordes of post-World War II

---

* Activity Vector Analysis—a personality test consisting of lists of words which a person might use to describe himself. The test produces scores in such areas as aggressiveness, sociability, emotional adjustment, social adaptability. At one time this test was widely marketed and used by innumerable blue chip corporations in their personnel procedure.

** Wonderlic—a short-form intelligence test not unlike the Otis Test of Mental Ability.

*** Klein—the Klein Institute for Aptitude Testing is a test bureau which screens job applicants through the use of psychological tests.

students, did those things most expedient just to process the numbers of students and companies from one day to the next. So, perhaps it is understandable why so little research, so little of an innovative nature has been forthcoming until the last half-dozen years. Even now not enough research is being done by placement directors themselves. A few anthropologists, sociologists, and psychologists have set forth mostly heuristic theories of guidance and vocational choice, primarily for the purpose of stimulating research and investigation which is urgently needed in the fields of vocational counseling and placement.

Current Theories of Vocational Choice

It is not the purpose of this chapter to become involved in an analysis of current theory. On the other hand, a brief survey of several of the more provocative heuristic theories will, perhaps, demonstrate how far thinking has come since the turn of the century, and at the same time point up the present need for research and the development of a body of knowledge in the area of vocational choice. John Holland, in summarizing the results of several decades of research in vocational choice, says that the best way to predict vocational choice is simply to ask a person what he wants to be. "Our best devices," says Holland, "do not exceed the predictive value of that method." [8] Holland, therefore, to stimulate investigation and research, poses the hypothesis that people search for environments and vocations that will enable them to role-play; he then categorizes most persons into one of six types in which they role-play: (1) realistic; (2) intellectual; (3) social; (4) conventional; (5) enterprising; and (6) artistic. Within the framework of this experimental theory, vocational choice would depend upon the extent to which that vocation enabled the individual to role-play his particular type.[8]

Another investigator, A. A. Brill, furnishes a psychoanalytic view of career choice. In essence, this theory suggests that there is always a psychic determinant of vocational choice. For example, the actor is sublimating exhibitionism into acting; feelings of guilt or remorse for real or imaginary sins are often the basis of theological callings.[9]

B. R. Forer suggests that vocational choice is not primarily rational or logical, but rather an impulsive, emotional, automatic process, a culmination of the individual's unique psychological development. Forer maintains with Brill that the primary reasons for career selection are unconscious in the sense that when an individual is pressed for reasons for a particular choice, he can give only the barest, most superficial rationalization such as, "he simply has to build bridges" or "he cannot stand paper work." [10]

John Darley has theorized that vocational interest types evolve with the development of personality.[11]

Considerable evidence exists [12] to the effect that occupational stereotyping affects vocational choice. E. S. Bordin has developed a series of hypotheses that relate to this concept. Vocational goals, he theorizes, as expressed on the vocational interest blank, set forth the individual's view of himself in terms of the particular vocational stereotypes he holds; the interest rating varies according to the degree with which the individual believes the occupational stereotype is self-descriptive.[13] Eli Ginzberg, S. W. Ginsburg, S. Axelrod, and J. L. Herma have developed a general theory which hypothesizes that occupational choice is a process which takes place over a period of 10 or more years. Further, they theorize that since each decision during adolescence is related to one's past experiences which, in turn, influence the future, the process of decision-making is irreversible. And, finally, since occupational choice involves weighing a number of subjective elements against the limitations of reality, occupational choice is always the result of compromise.[14]

Maslow,[15] Roe,[16] and Schaffer [17] each have common elements in their respective theories of basic needs and their relation to vocational choice. They conceive job choice as the satisfaction of certain basic needs of the human organism; such needs are defined as physiological needs, the need for importance, respect, self-esteem, independence, self-actualization, etc. Within the last few years Super's developmental theory of choice has enjoyed an increasing acceptance. Super is critical of the term "vocational choice" for the reason that the very tenor suggests that at some point in time a vocational decision is made. Super, together with an increasing number of counselors, believes that vocational choice is "a process rather than an event," the end product of the development of an individual's ideas, ideals, attitudes, interests, experiences, and abilities over a considerable period of time. Super divides the developmental process into a series of life stages: (1) growth; (2) exploratory; (3) establishment; (4) maintenance; (5) decline. Throughout these stages, the process of vocational development is essentially that of developing and implementing a self-concept. Within the framework of such a concept, work satisfaction is dependent upon adequate opportunities to develop interests, to sharpen abilities, to refine personality traits, to develop a system of values—all of which become ingredients of one's concept of self.[17a]

There is a growing body of evidence that career choice is developmental, that early environmental influences play a profound role not only in shaping personality, intellectual and emotional growth, but also in shaping the individual's value scheme. From early elementary school age throughout one's educational development, an endless array of factors determine value goals which, in turn, ultimately affect vocational choice: play experiences, how one's early needs were satisfied or not satisfied, teachers, parental attitudes and prejudices, newspapers, television, part-time jobs, and hobbies—just to mention a few.

In a 1965 study of "Career Choices of Successful Business Executives" by Harold Hubbard,[18] it was found that business executives ranked the greatest influences on their decision to enter business in the following order: (1) family, personal friends, and admired persons; (2) books, periodicals, and magazines; (3) high school and college courses; and (4) motion pictures, fraternal relationships, and career-oriented organizations.

It should be noted that the business executives in this sample had a median age of 47 years; yet they felt the *frappé de force* of their vocational decisions was rooted in the early years of their lives.

Another study of Gribbons and Lohnes [19] concludes that "self-concept systems . . . are crucial in determining occupational preferences . . . and that data show a maturity of self-concepts early in the eighth grade—sufficient to justify close attention from counselors at that time . . ." This study further indicates that "it has been shown that school counselors can interfere successfully in the vocational process . . . (by) "assisting young people at an early age to an increased awareness of their personal value hierarchies, to the improvement of their values, and to the integration of their values, their aspirations, and their plans."

A very provocative article in the December 1966 issue of the *Vocational Guidance Quarterly* on "Vocational Development: Theory and Practice" [20] is essential reading for any serious practitioner of vocational counseling. Therein Robert Wurtz calls attention to the fact that ". . . the individual develops bit by bit. Each step . . . not only has bearing on, but indeed is, the basis of each succeeding stage . . . Thus the nature of development in each stage . . . is determined by prior ones (stages) . . . No one can . . . delineate . . . what the individual should become and then grow him into it." Wurtz discusses the folly of setting up goals in guidance, reminding us of the mother whose son is going to college or else! And the boy who struggles with mathematics because he wants to become an engineer. Such attempts to manipulate the developmental process in terms of goal orientation alone fail. "Implementing a self-concept," says Wurtz, "requires that one know the self, a particularly difficult task when the self is still developing."

A point to consider here, as counselors, is how valid is an occupationally oriented approach to counseling. When students are referred to occupational literature, to think in terms of job goals, they are not being encouraged to look at themselves. Underlying any such approach, says Wurtz, "must be the tacit assumption that (1) the normal evolutionary process of development will lead to this occupation, or (2) the developmental process can be manipulated . . ."

The question, then, here becomes "Can development be manipulated?" Gribbons and Lohnes say it can; others say it cannot. This bit of controversy is reported to indicate to the reader the state of flux in which vocational counseling and placement are found today—a good pace from the security of the Parsons hypothesis, yet an equally good distance from a discipline supported by a body of demonstrable facts. Perhaps one of the reasons why the student is alienated from the counselor is that the student is not convinced the counselor really knows what he is doing. How does one build bridges without basic proven engineering theory on which to hang the facts? How does one develop a financial statement without a framework of accounting theory? How can one counsel without the support of a body of proven theory?

Concerning this position, Anne Roe says:

> "It has become abundantly clear that the problem of occupational adjustment is not merely one of matching aptitudes or even patterns of aptitudes to established job requirements for these aptitudes (although this is not excluded) but that it is as complicated as life adjustment, of which it is only a facet. We are just beginning to learn techniques of study which will throw light on the intricate relationships involved. This suggests that for some time to come we shall need the most painstaking and intensive studies . . ." [21]

There are other concerns which confront the career counselor these days. One very basic question is how long can he continue to fragmentize counseling into separate areas of personal, educational, and vocational counseling? After all, counselors are dealing with individuals who are whole persons; the educational pattern which they follow and the ultimate vocations which they will pursue surely must be the end products of their value systems, their educational achievements, and their responses and adjustments to a variety of environmental stimuli. Must not the counselor of tomorrow, then, be the counselor of the whole individual? And how best does one counsel the individual?

What kind of professional preparation will best prepare the counselor for the role he will play? Answers to this question are now being sought both by the College Placement Council and the American College Personnel Association. Even when professional criteria are established, since the profession is so young and so dynamic, there is little doubt that professional educational requirements will remain in a state of flux for some time to come. At a conference held at Columbia University in 1964 under the auspices of the Division of Counseling Psychology of the American Psychological Association to discuss counselor preparation, there was a consensus that courses in personality development and dynamics, clinical techniques, and special knowledge and skills in educational and career counseling are basic to counselor education. Some placement practitioners today, while they have the wisdom of experience, lack the formal educational requirements. Unless placement directors give serious direction to their professionalization, standards may well be dictated by "outsiders"—namely counseling psychologists, clinical psychologists, and psychiatrists. The day of the placement "traffic officer" and the "bureau of appointments" is gone forever.

Yet another stupendous problem faces the career counselor: the growing student population, the numbers game. How best shall he, for surely he will, make the computer his servant? The day is close at hand when the average small college will be able to have on-line access to a computer. The time is also nearer than one might guess when it will be possible to feed into the machine such information as grades, achievement test results, personality traits, interest and aptitude appraisals, along with case histories and counselor judgments, and have the computer match these against qualities sought by companies in their search for job candidates. The computer will do two things of especial importance for the counselor: (1) it will free the counselor so he can counsel; and (2) it will become an invaluable aid in developing some long overdue, sophisticated research in career counseling. Of course, the machine will create some knotty problems, too; one of the more serious problems will be how individuality is to be both served and preserved.

Or what about this problem? Might there not be value in a required (credit or non-credit) course in self-understanding, goal development, and career planning—call it what you will? The object of such a course would be to "know thyself." In this course one might explore societal, corporate, and individual values, establish personal value goals, become involved in some self-measurement of a psychological nature, acquire pertinent occupational information and learn something about the world of work. Already one can hear the cries of faculty colleagues, many of whom probably drifted into teaching by default because they had no real knowledge of anything else. A required course in individual development and career orientation could be one of the most valuable courses in a college curriculum.

There are myriad other problems that confront the career counselor such as the placement of minority groups, how best to aid the disadvantaged, what to do about the physically and emotionally handicapped, the ethical and legal implications of student freedoms in placement procedures, the meaning of work in an affluent society, etc. Concerning the problem of counseling in a changing world, Joseph Kauffman has this to say, ". . . we live in an era when this noble enterprise is termed 'computerized universities,' when too many faculty are referred to as 'entrepreneurs,' deans as 'cops,' registrars and admissions officers as 'petty bureaucrats'—and I have even noted the reference to counseling as a 'rat-fink' operation." [22]

The loss of faith on the part of students in counselors at the secondary school level seems to have impact on behavior toward counselors at the college level; many college students never bother to investigate the counseling resources available to them in college. Student after student surveyed in an 18-

college study by Arnold, Stevens, and Stephens in 1965–66 revealed that "he never had any contact with the counseling services, or that he doesn't even know where the placement office is." [23] One may well ask the question, "Why?"

Max Lerner may have some of the answers:

> "The test of a society may, from one angle of vision, be the kind of questions that it asks—not the overt but the covert questions, not just those we teach and preach but those we live. I remember stopping at the window of a New York shop once, my attention caught by a sign on display: 'If you're so smart, why aren't you rich?' That was one I could not answer, and after standing for a long time looking at it I walked away. But I was like a chicken fascinated by a snake, and I came back. Finally with a sigh of relief I had the answer: the answer was that it was the wrong question.
>
> "We ask a good many wrong questions in our society. Perhaps on university campuses here and there some of the right questions are beginning to be asked. There is the question of *emergence:* What kind of a personality can I shape, in what kind of possible society? There is the question of *access:* Am I helping give others a chance at life— equal to my own? There are questions of *selfhood:* Who am I? What are my threads of connection with my family, my community, my country, my fellow human beings? There are questions of *transcendence:* Do I dare make the journey into the interior which is the most dangerous journey of all? Do I dare confront what I find there and go beyond it? Do I dare face tragedy without being destroyed by it? There are questions of *commitment:* Do I have work I care about? Am I capable of play, of giving and receiving love, of taking risks for goals I value? Can I explore the depths

and heights of joyousness? Finally there is the question of *nexus:* Does my society have in it the stuff of cohesiveness? Do I have a sense of the human connection, in the sure knowledge that what happens to others happens thereby also to me?" [24]

In dealing with students it is important to remember that it is not what the facts really are, but, rather, what students think the facts are. Students think they have been neglected, that they have lost their identity, that the values of yesterday are useless today. How will student personnel workers respond to this kind of student thinking?

One thing seems certain as one looks into the future of counseling: the counselor had better be a flexible personality, for change will be the order of the future.

BIBLIOGRAPHY

1 Cowley, W. H., "Some History and a Venture in Prophecy," an essay in *Trends in Student Personnel Work,* E. G. Williamson, Univ. Minn. Press, Minneapolis, 1949, p. 20.

2 Ibid., p. 20.

3 Mueller, Kate H., *Student Personnel Work in Higher Education,* Houghton Mifflin, Boston, 1961, pp. 52–53.

4 Eliot, Charles W., "Undesirable and Desirable Uniformity in Schools," *Proceedings of the N.E.A.,* 1892, p. 83.

5 Dewey, John, *The Child and The Curriculum,* U. Chicago Press, Chicago, 1902, pp. 13–14.

6 Mueller, ibid., p. 54.

7 Parsons, Frank, *Choosing a Vocation,* Houghton Mifflin, Boston, 1909, pp. 4–5.

8 Holland, John L., "A Theory of Vocational Choice," *Vocational Guidance Quarterly,* Summer 1963, Vol. II, #4, pp. 23 ff.

9 Brill, A. A., *Basic Principles of Psychoanalysis,* Doubleday & Co., Inc., Garden City, N.Y., 1949.

10 Forer, B. R., "Personality Factors in Occupational Choice," *Educational and Psychological Measurement,* Autumn 1953, p. 361.

11 Roe, Anne, *The Psychology of Occupations,* John Wiley & Sons, Inc., N.Y., 1966, p. 268.

12 Arnold, Dorothy L., Stevens, Nancy D., and Stephens, Everett W., "What Are the Attitudes of Students Toward Occupations?," *Journal of College Placement,* December 1966–January 1967.

13 Roe, Anne, ibid., pp. 268–269.

14 Ginzberg, E. W., S. W. Ginsburg, S. Axelrod, J. L. Herma, *Occupational Choice—An Approach to a General Theory,* Columbia U. Press, N.Y., 1951.

15 Maslow, A. H., *Motivation and Personality,* Harper & Row, Inc., N.Y., 1954.

16 Roe, Anne, ibid., pp. 31 ff.

17 Schaffer, R. H., "Job Satisfaction as Related to Need Satisfaction in Work," *Psychological Monographs,* #364, 1953, p. 1.

17a Super, D.E. and Bachrach, P.B., "Scientific Careers and Vocational Development Theory," Columbia University, Teachers College Bureau of Publications, N.Y., 1957.

18 Hubbard, H. G., "Career Choices of Successful Business Executives," *Personnel and Guidance Journal,* October 1965, p. 149.

19 Gribbons, Warren D., and Lohnes, Paul R., "Shifts in Adolescents' Values," *Personnel and Guidance Journal,* Nov., 1965, pp. 248 ff.

20 Wurtz, Robert E., "Vocational Development: Theory and Practice," *Vocational Guidance Quarterly,* December 1966, pp. 127 ff.

21 Roe, ibid., p. 314.

22 Kauffman, Joseph F., *"The Time of the Student: Shall We Overcome?,"* an essay in *The College and The Student,* American Council on Education, Washington, D. C., 1966, p. 389.

23 Arnold, Stevens, and Stephens, ibid., p. 10.

24 Lerner, Max, "The Revolutionary Frame of Our Time," an essay in *The College and The Student,* American Council on Education, Washington, D. C., 1966, p. 22.

CHAPTER 2

Placement— A Developing Profession

Changing Concepts in Placement

I T IS FORTUNATE that placement had its start with a practical crew at the helm. For the most part, placement officers have been able to relate readily to company recruiters and to industry in general. They have spoken both the language of the students and of industry. Undoubtedly, one of placement's greatest contributions is the development of strong industry-education ties. In this respect, placement offices have served the college, the student, and employers well in the post-World War II years.

Today marked changes can be seen throughout education, including placement. The age of affluence, the philosophy of education for all, the increasing emphasis on graduate study and the lack of need of many to become economically independent early in life, the growing number of frustrated, fragmented personalities created by our dichotomous value system and their need for counsel and guidance as a prerequisite to career planning—these and many other highly dynamic factors are presenting higher education with a variety of challenges. Among the challenges which directly affect the placement office are the large numbers of students needing pre-placement counseling together with the large numbers going on to graduate school.

Today many are not impressed by the size of the starting salaries of big business. Many react violently to quantification and depersonalization. Some are not much impressed by the high aims and noble purposes of education. They are searching for meaning in their lives, and they are not quite sure what they want. Youth needs more than job interviews. They need understanding counsel that will help them arrive at meaningful value systems, help that will enable them to crystallize their goals. In addition to help in finding a job, there is great need for considerable counseling and guidance before meaningful career planning can become a reality. According to several studies [1, 2, 3] students are seeking such advice and counsel primarily from faculty and family, not from counseling services and placement.

Such a trend is raising serious questions among college administrators, particularly in the small liberal arts colleges, about the need for an employment-type of placement office. Harold W. Stoke, in his book *The American College President*,[4] asks: "Are we running a welfare operation in the placement office, or is there genuine extra-classroom, extra-academic learning going on?" Is there?

Dr. Nancy Stevens [5] forewarned in the June 1965 *Journal of College Student Personnel* that the placement service must become a functional part of the total educational process. She noted that, increasingly, placement directors are becoming less interested in the number of placements counted each year, and more interested in the number of students whom they are able to counsel and guide in their career planning. Her own college placement office (Hunter), under the leadership of Dr. Alva C. Cooper, long ago became the Office of Career Counseling and Placement. A scattering of other colleges across the country have sensed the trend as well. Their change in orientation is reflected in recent name changes from "Placement Office" to

"Office of Career Counseling," "Office of Career Planning," "Office of Vocational Guidance and Placement"—to mention a few.

With this change, Stevens [5] warns that counseling and guidance require some specialized knowledge and skills which some placement officers concerned mainly with employment may not possess.

The Need to Professionalize

There is a shocking dearth of research and writing on placement in the journals and periodicals published in the past 40 years. The same can be said of textbooks. Even a text like May Brunson's *Guidance, An Integrating Process in Higher Education* [6] makes no mention of placement. Why not? Where have placement educators been? What have they been doing?

Joseph Samler, speaking at the fiftieth anniversary celebration of the National Vocational Guidance Association in Boston in 1963, observed:

> "The argument that the counselor must be technically competent cannot be countered . . . There is only one answer, really. The counselor must be well trained, competent, able to understand current work applying to his field, whether this is in the appreciation of developmental stages, close knowledge of the labor market, the nuances of the self-concept, the use of TAT, the applicability of x^2, or whatever . . . What is puzzling is why we have to defend this position. We'd be pretty impatient with a dishwasher service man who started fumbling around and did not know how to get the front panel off the dishwasher, or how to replace the water pump. We would not brook argument about the unacceptability of a social studies teacher who does not know the his-

tory of the relationship of the federal government to the states, but somehow we continue to have to knock ourselves out to define the need for the counselor to know his trade. What is wrong with us?" [7]

No one is so naive as to believe that all professional preparation is formal classroom learning. Experience counts a great deal. However, the point is that if placement is ever going to become a profession in the true sense of the word, a start must be made with the education of those who would join the "profession." Placement personnel cannot let their own heterogeneous backgrounds, perhaps even their feelings of insecurity, cloud the issue. They have to start sometime, somewhere.

Let us take a look, then, at what professionalizing would mean to student personnel educators involved in placement.

What Makes One Professional?

Dr. Alan Klass (an M.D.) writing in the *Northwest Engineer* [8] borrowed a definition of the word "profession" from an article by one P. Wright in the *Canadian Bar Review*.[9] Borrowing from both of these gentlemen, this definition emerges: "A profession is a self-selected, self-disciplined group of individuals who hold themselves out to the public as possessing a special skill derived from education and training and who are prepared to exercise that skill primarily in the interests of others."

The *Dictionary of Education* [10] defines a profession as an occupation that requires relatively long and specialized preparation on the higher education level and that is governed by a special code of ethics. Roscoe Pound once defined a profession as "an organized calling in which men pursue a learned art and are united in the pursuit of public service." [11]

The professions of medicine, law, and religion set up rigid standards of education; to gain the inner circle, examinations revealing knowledge of standards must be passed. Once within the circle, ethical codes of conduct must be adhered to. Failure to live up to professional standards leads to being defrocked, disbarred, or having one's right to practice revoked. This is what professionalization is all about.

If one is honest about the matter, while some individuals in placement could measure up to the implied educational requirements of the definitions, placement personnel in general lack special and common skills; they do not practice an art held in common. It is fair to say that placement has not yet achieved the status of a profession.

What, then, are the steps to be taken to become professional? Several tasks of considerable magnitude confront placement if it is to achieve the status of a profession: (1) the establishment of educational standards, both pre-professional and graduate; (2) the development of a body of specialized knowledge; (3) the establishment and maintenance of standards of admission to the profession and standards of performance in the profession; (4) the development of and adherence to a code of ethics; (5) establishment of screening measures to help assure that practitioners will be individuals capable of developing meaningful, warm, and effective interpersonal relationships with clients; in short, the professional counselor will be more interested in ends (people) than means to ends (techniques). Placement has a real job to do to implement such tasks.

The Establishment of Educational Standards

It seems reasonable to require members of a like profession to have common educational backgrounds within a broad framework of offerings. The minimum educational requirement might be the master's degree. As in medicine, pre-professional work had best be broad. However, major work in the areas of anthropology, psychology, and sociology would be most beneficial; the ability to communicate in English is essential.

The graduate professional program certainly should include broad understandings in such areas as the following: (1) psychology, including individual development, personality development, and abnormal psychology; (2) theories of vocational development; (3) administering and interpreting psychological tests and measurements; (4) occupational information; (5) the labor market; (6) counseling theory, techniques, and practice; (7) theories of group dynamics; (8) educational statistics; (9) computer applications to personnel management; (10) personnel research techniques; and (11) placement office operations.

Development of Specialized Knowledge

While the *Fundamentals of College Placement* (College Placement Council, 1962) pioneered in consolidating information relative to the operation of a placement office, this text is the first to include substantive information about career counseling, guidance, and placement. There is need for additional information about developmental biology and psychology, for example, that makes possible an individual's effective performance as a counselor. Vast amounts of research must be done because, for the most part, placement operates on a set of unproven assumptions about human behavior and vocational choice. While placement counselors may borrow much from their colleagues in counseling, they need, through studies and research, to establish a body of proven behavior principles on which the foundation of professional knowledge can be built. Only then can placement become professional.

The College Placement Council Foundation, established in 1968, is intended to encourage such study and research so badly needed.

Professional Standards

The adoption of any set of professional standards must have a "grandfather" or escape clause. Of course, all the placement personnel presently employed across the country should not be dismissed just because their educational backgrounds may not meet proposed minimum professional standards. The problem is that placement must start somewhere, sometime. And the time is now.

It can be assumed, then, that credit will be given for experience. In addition the College Placement Council, through universities and regional associations, could offer regular seminars to update its membership professionally, thereby helping fill the void in educational background of some, and keeping all abreast of the latest in theory and practice. A start has already been made by several regional placement associations with their professional workshops.

Placement officers already subscribe to a code of ethics, *The Principles and Practices of College Placement and Recruitment* (see Chapter 10). This instrument was developed originally by the College Placement Council in cooperation with the Chamber of Commerce of the United States. The code has helped to assure ethical behavior on the part of placement personnel, student job hunters, and employers. This code was updated in 1964, restructured in 1968, and updated once again in 1970. Acceptance of the code is a condition of membership in almost all regional placement associations.

Interest in People vs. Techniques

The technical requirements of the degree or the mastering of clinical techniques are far less important qualities needed in a counselor than warmth and an understanding personality— the ability to relate to others. Too often on too many campuses one finds superb, technically competent Ph.D.s totally incapable of relating to much else than their statistics. Hopefully, if professional standards are established, one will be able to find both the technically competent and warm, understanding personality wrapped up in the same package.

Gardner Murphy [12] out of his years of experience said that there is not enough attention being given to personality and interpersonal relationships in the selection of counselors. Rather, too much attention is being given to craft skills. The basic issue, as he saw it, is personality versus technique.

It is to be hoped that in any standards which may develop in the profession, the personality of the counselor will be carefully examined.

Implications of Attempts to Professionalize

Professionalization of student personnel educators in placement will not be an easy task for it is fraught with problems.

Problem 1—Attitudes of College Presidents Toward Placement.

Too many college presidents have failed to perceive the role of the placement director as professional. On many campuses, placement personnel have been recruited without adequate educational and experience backgrounds. They, therefore, have difficulty relating to counseling. The college president has too often seen the placement office only as a place where space is made available to companies for interviews; some faculty and students have seen it the same way. It is encouraging to note, however, that other college presidents have taken steps to strengthen the counseling aspects of placement.

Even if all placement workers were to agree on the need to professionalize, a serious bottleneck could be the president's office. There is, therefore, an urgent need, concurrent with any attempt to professionalize, to "educate" college presidents.

Problem 2—Lethargy.

The one greatest obstacle to professionalization may be the lethargy of placement workers themselves. Because they are overworked and understaffed, as few other college personnel, little time is left for "cerebrating," for contemplating, for research, or for writing. Theirs so often is the philosophy of expediency—get done today what I must, for the pile on the desk grows ever larger.

Unless one gives some thought to the need to professionalize, unless one takes the time to communicate, unless one as a result of his reading and communication and thoughtful deliberation knows why he must professionalize, and the consequences if he does not, action is not likely to come about.

It is hoped that the leadership offered by the College Placement Council on this and other equally important issues will be accepted.

Problem 3—Professionalization and the United States Employment Service.

From 1962–1964 nationwide concern was expressed by placement associations and by the College Placement Council over the strong interest in the college placement function shown by USES. Indeed, in a few colleges across the country, college presidents were convinced that USES could run the placement offices better than the college might. In a handful of colleges, USES still operates these placement offices.

One of the strong arguments in 1962–1964 against the use of USES staff was the lack of educational qualifications of its employees to do the job. Since that time USES has been busy putting its house in order. The Service is seeking funds to promote grants for the training of 1,000 counselors per year at the master's degree level. The training proposed includes a broad knowledge of psychology, counseling techniques, test administration, interpretation of the labor market and occupational information, social psychology, theories of vocational choice, and industrial psychology.

Further, USES was instrumental in establishing a new employment counseling division within the American Personnel and Guidance Association, the National Employment Counselors Association.

There is little doubt that by 1975 USES will have adopted a set of minimum professional standards and will have counselors prepared to handle college placement activities.

How will placement directors, regional associations, and the College Placement Council confront this development?

Problem 4—Need for Implementation of National Standards.

It is a fairly reasonable assumption that there cannot be a variety of professional standards espoused by various regional associations. It seems logical to propose national professional standards, if any at all. And if this is to be accomplished, reasonable individuals know that they will be called upon to make individual sacrifices here and there for the greater common good.

There will be problems in developing professionally, and at the same time retaining regional autonomy. It is commendable that none of the regions wants to become part of a large national association, so mammoth and so impersonal that the regional associations might lose their effectiveness.

Yet, if placement is to move forward with the times, some way must be found to implement national standards. It is hoped by many that the College Placement Council can be developed into a kind of regional associations senate, empowered in accordance with the direction given by the various regional senate members. Placement—the future well-being of all those involved in placement—will be exactly what placement educators and their regional associations make of it. Is placement ready for such action?

BIBLIOGRAPHY

[1] Arnold, Dorothy L. and Stevens, Nancy D. and Stephens, Everett W., "What Are the Attitudes of Students Toward Occupations," *Journal of College Placement*, Dec. 1966–Jan. 1967.

[2] Calvert, Jr. Robert, from a study of 11,000 male graduates under a $92,000 grant from the Coop. Research Division of U.S. Office of Education conducted through the Survey Research Center, U. Cal.

[3] Stephens, Everett W. and Stevens, Nancy D. "What Are the Factors Influencing the Attitudes of Students Toward Occupations?," *Journal of College Placement*, March 1968.

4 Stoke, Harold W., "The American College President," Harper, New York, 1958.

5 Stevens, Nancy D., "A Changing Concept of College Placement," *Journal of College Student Personnel*, VI, June 1965, p. 233.

6 Brunson, May, "Guidance, An Integrating Process in Higher Education."

7 Samler, Joseph—in an address given before the 50th anniversary celebration of the National Vocational Guidance Association, April 1963, Boston, Mass.

8 Klass, Alan, from an essay in the *Northwest Engineer*, Vol. XVI, No. 3, May–June 1962.

9 Wright, P., From an article in the *Canadian Bar Review*, Vol. XXIX, 1951, p. 748.

10 *Dictionary of Education*, McGraw-Hill Book Co., N.Y., 1939, p. 18.

11 Pound, Roscoe, "What Is a Profession?" *Review of Reviews*, XCIV, 1936, pp. 84–85.

12 Murphy, Gardner, "The Cultural Context of Guidance," *Personnel and Guidance Journal*, Vol. 34, No. 1, Sept. 1955, pp. 4 ff.

CHAPTER 3

Developing a Philosophy
of Career Counseling

WHAT, AMIDST REVOLUTIONARY change, can a placement director believe? Are there enduring principles to guide his thinking? Are there proven practices?

There is a handful of abiding principles, both psychologically and educationally sound, which can guide placement practices and influence change. It is the purpose of this chapter to set forth these principles and their implications in practice.

Principle 1—The aim of higher education is the development of whole individuals equipped to cope with a fast-changing world.

Implications of Principle 1—Individual development implies individual differences. Hence, if the placement educator subscribes to Principle 1, then he recognizes that each individual is a unique personality with a particular combination of interests, abilities, personality traits, scheme of values, etc. And if our society is to be creative, productive, and satisfying for the individual, educators must recognize, encourage, develop, and respect differences among individuals.

Another implication of the "whole-individual" concept is that placement must be concerned about educating whole individuals, not fragmented individuals. As whole individuals, the students to be counseled, then, are considerably more than job hunters, potential employees; they are at one and the same time potential husbands, wives, fathers, or mothers, town-meeting members, Little League coaches, consumers, world travelers, voters, taxpayers, and citizens of a world community as well as breadwinners.

By the same reasoning, they must become more than perennial students. Whole individuals will understand the economic role they will play in our culture. If, indeed, the college takes its responsibility seriously in helping to develop whole individuals, then that college will be as concerned about the vocational implication of higher education as it is about the cultural heritage. A college which boasts of its ability to sharpen the intellects of its students but dodges the responsibility of educating a student in the understanding of himself and how he may relate to the world of work in the Twentieth Century is not really developing whole individuals.

There is general agreement today about the need for breadth of education even in our technical institutions, schools of education, and colleges of business administration. There is, however, concern on the part of many that more of our liberal arts institutions need to climb up out of the Eighteenth Century and confront their students with a Twentieth Century world. Any liberal institution which seriously relates its learnings to the Twentieth Century cannot escape in the classroom or in its counseling the vocational implications of its educational offerings.

There is another implication of Principle 1 which deserves comment and with which few as yet have had much experience. It is quite possible that a counselee, a product of the age of affluence, finds it increasingly difficult to fulfill his self-concept primarily in the role of work. With the fading of the long-held, puritanical belief in the virtues of hard work, fulfillment may come via becoming the fastest skier on the slope or the breeziest sailor along the coast or, perhaps, a knowledgeable traveler. Employment, in an age of plenty, and particularly as our society moves into an ever shorter work week, and as the machine contributes more to our decision-making, takes on different meaning. In such a context, the motivation of vocational choice today will be vastly different from the motivational factors in time of depression or war economy.

Adoption of the "whole-individual" philosophy will guide the counselor in his relation to the counselee. The "whole-individual" philosophy will envision career counseling as something vastly more than job counseling; placement cannot, then, stop with occupational information and arranging interviews. Placement cannot stop with psychological testing for interests, abilities, and personality traits. Placement must go all the way in counseling the whole individual; and if placement personnel are lacking in the educational preparation or experience to counsel broadly, then channels will be developed and kept open with campus counseling services. Placement will then become a cooperative venture with the college counseling services.

Principle 2—Growth is a developmental process.

Recent research suggests that individuals proceed through a variety of stages physically, emotionally, intellectually, and vocationally. This is known as growth. Development, while it relates somewhat to chronological age, is generally a matter of individual differences. Maturation follows an orderly developmental sequence from a prenatal period through old age. The Gesell [1] studies, for example, found that the average, 4-week-old infant cannot hold his head up or sit up, nor will he respond to visual stimuli. However, as the child develops, at 16 weeks, on the average, he can hold his head steady; and at 36 weeks the infant can sit erect for as much as 10 minutes. At the end of 2 years, the same infant is able to run without falling down.

There is a continuum of development within a broad time reference: between 6 and 12, one learns physical skills necessary for a variety of games, develops skills in reading, writing, and numbers, and becomes sensitive to conscience, moral values, and social attitudes. From 12 to 18, one learns to accept his particular sex role, develops intellectual skills, strives for independence, and flirts with imaginary occupational roles. From 18 to 35, development involves selecting a marriage partner, beginning a family, and exploring a tentative occupational role. The years from 35 to 60 are years of vocational stabilization.

John Piaget[2] believes that each step in cognitive growth makes the next step possible. It is known from a variety of studies, too, that growth is discontinuous; that is, sometimes there are spurts and at other times lags in development. Growth is uneven.

One, then, does not suddenly walk or talk or fear dogs or hate Martians. Learnings, attitudes, values develop slowly as reactions to environmental stimuli. Likewise, there is evidence that career choice is not a decision which is reached at a certain point in time. The evidence is strong that vocational choice is the sum of a variety of environmental influences reaching well back into the early years, a developmental process.

In his theory of vocational development, Super[3] conceives of "vocational development . . . as one aspect of individual development . . . Like other aspects of development (it) . . . may be conceived of as beginning early in life and as proceeding along a curve until late in life. Thus the 4-year-old who plays carpenter or storekeeper is in a very early stage of vocational development, and the septuagenarian who no longer teaches or does research but still attends scientific meetings or writes his professional autobiography is in a very late stage of vocational development . . ."

Implications of Principle 2—If it is true that growth is developmental, the selection of a career, then, is not something that happens at a point in time. Environmental influences and developmental opportunities for students become of prime concern to the placement director. His part-time job service will take on new significance as a potent factor in growth. Summer experiences and extracurricular activities take on new dimensions. The need for a variety of materials in an occupational library, and more important, the need to relate these to college majors and to have the library used become important issues in individual development. Concern over use of the vocational library and its development can lead to the establishment of a strong working relationship with department heads.

When the developmental approach to career counseling is taken, there is the realization that the sooner contact is made with the college student the more ready he may be to make a job choice in the senior year. Hence, counseling freshmen and programs of service for freshmen become necessities.

Principle 3—Successful vocational choice lies in fulfilling the self-concept.

Over the years psychologists have had the urge to raise chimpanzees from birth in order to compare their development and growth with *homo sapiens*. Robert and Ada Yerkes succeeded in raising a chimp along with their infant son. In their early stages of development, for nearly a year, the chimp and the child demonstrated an almost parallel development. But from the second year on, marked changes occurred in the human infant that separated him forever from the anthropoid. The child began to refer to himself as an "I," and, in fact, emerged from being a little animal to becoming a person. It is this consciousness of self that shapes man's whole personality structure and makes him a unique individual.

It is within the concept of self that the individual holds his aspirations and ideals, his values and goals. It is in the self-concept that the individual sees himself as he thinks he is. Individual fulfillment is found through becoming what one would have oneself become. A person's self-concept generally remains constant, and considerable effort is expended both consciously and unconsciously to maintain the image that has developed over the years.

Tightly bound up in this self-concept are one's vocational ambitions and goals. One sees oneself in the service of others, as the entrepreneur, as the researcher of the unknown. Fulfillment of the self-concept through vocational choice is essential to the well-being and happiness of the organism.

Implications of Principle 3—If one of man's basic psychological needs is self-fulfillment in terms of the self-concept, and if there is a psychological homeostasis which motivates behavior to maintain intact the self-image, it is especially important that the career counselor be knowledgeable in developmental psychology and psychology of personality. The understanding of personality and its role in motivating occupational choice is basic to all other counseling activities. Occupational information, advisement, and counseling will, then, fall within the frame of reference of the self-concept.

Principle 4—Counseling is the heart of the placement function.

The placement office of tomorrow, with the sharply spiraling increase in college and university budgets, will be called upon to justify its existence. The occupational information functions in a job brokerage operation might be maintained by the campus library. And the arrangement of job interviews, in a brokerage operation, might well be done by competent secretaries. What, then, is important in placement? It is the counseling function.

Implications of Principle 4—The career counselor can be of especial value in helping students understand themselves in relation to the world of work. Vocational growth can thereby be stimulated.

Some placement educators, frustrated by their experiences in trying to reach the student who most needs help but never seeks it, have advocated either a credit or non-credit course in "Occupational Development and Growth of the Individual." It seems illogical that higher education, which today demands such breadth of knowledge of its students, includes in the curricula few, if any, courses that might give students understanding of themselves.

Placement could make a much needed contribution to the education of the college student by lobbying for course work along the lines of "Occupational Development and Growth of the Individual." Such a course might include subject matter in human development and growth (physical, psychological, emotional, vocational); theories of personality; the self-concept; the relationship of aptitudes, interests, and personality traits to occupational choice; and occupational information. Hopefully, such a course of study would set the stage for a more effective utilization by the student of placement office resources.

Principle 5—The effectiveness of a placement service can be measured by its educational value to the student and to the college.

Implications of Principle 5—The *raison d'être* of an educational institution is to educate. Some college placement offices are exciting places of learning on campus; others are dead and do not know it! The office that advises but offers little counseling and guidance is obviously of less educational value to the student than the office that both counsels and guides. And the office that has built an extensive library of occupational information but has not yet found ways to get the library into the hands of the students is really of little educational value to anyone. Likewise, the bureau-of-appointments job-brokerage type operation really offers little of educational value—either to the student or the college.

The placement office which becomes involved in teaching, counseling, guidance, and research is the office which has the potential to cause students to think about themselves, to begin to tackle the problem of how they relate to the world of work, and to come up with an array of solutions to that problem. Something of educational value is going on there.

Principle 6—The placement office functions primarily to serve the student.

Student-faculty relationships today often lack warmth and depth; they remain on the surface—cool, objective. Perhaps, because of his very numbers, the student remains more of a number than a person. And young people today are not what they used to be. Thank heavens! They were roughed up morally, if not physically, by Korea, Mississippi, Selma, Watts, Detroit, and Vietnam. And out of it all boils the need for treating the individual with dignity and understanding, as a person who counts, not another number to be fed to the prospective employer.

Counseling is a one-to-one process, a person-to-person relationship. It can be no other way. Career counseling puts the student first; it is concerned with the total development of the student, his welfare and happiness.

Implications of Principle 6—This point of view places the employer immediately in a certain perspective—in a secondary relationship to the placement office. The serious company field trips have their value; funds for the establishment of scholarship and/or the endowment of faculty chairs are all worthwhile public relations projects, but they cannot and must not influence the placement director to do other than be of service to the student.

It is important for career counseling personnel to become specialists in occupational information and to know as much as possible about prospective employers. As important as the development of good relationships between education and industry may be, the office of career counseling is not a public relations office; its job is student relations.

Principle 7—No one particular professional group is best qualified to counsel.

A division of labor in specialized student personnel services, as in medicine, is essential; but these specialists and their counseling must be held together by mutual respect and by common principles and practices which foster the best development of whole individuals.

Implications of Principle 7—From its very beginnings, placement has suffered from feelings of inferiority. Perhaps these feelings have not lessened because so little has been done by the profession to remove the causes of inferiority. And perhaps the counseling and clinical psychologists have developed feelings of superiority because they have worked at remaining superior. Perhaps.

The fact remains, as anyone who has done serious counseling knows, and as the student who is on the receiving end is well aware, the personality of the counselor and his ability to relate to his counselee are vastly more important than his degree of specialization in the art of counseling.

On the one hand, the clinician who becomes involved in techniques often fails to relate to the student; on the other hand, the placement director, because of his ignorance of the psychological implications, may fail to understand the significance of childhood experiences in the development of self-concept and its impact on vocational choice. Either way the student gets short-changed.

The counseling psychologist and the placement director can close the gap in their purposes and their learnings and work together in a common cause; there must develop a greater effort to understand one another, and a deeper respect for one another. The day will come, for it must, when one set of professional standards will prevail for all.

Principle 8—In dealing with students, it is important to remember that it is not what the facts are but, rather, what students think they are that will spell success or failure for the college administrator.

Most college administrators are aware of the ambivalent behavior of college students. Within this framework today is the earnest student yearning to develop individual freedoms for all; but at the same time some of these same students will go to great ends—unlawful if necessary—in preventing fellow students the freedom to have job interviews with allegedly controversial employers.

Implications of Principle 8—It is important for those dealing with college youth to be aware of this ever present ambivalence of facts versus what students think the facts are. When applied to counseling and placement activities, some interesting logic develops. For example, studies reveal that students struggle to gain independence from parents, and, in fact, think their parents pretty humdrum and not really very knowledgeable; at the same time, research reveals that it is the parents who are most influential in career choice. The same studies also reveal that the career counseling department which has a well-stocked vocational library and a strong staff of counselors is carefully avoided in the solution of personal and vocational problems.

Knowledge that this is how students are should challenge the wits of every college administrator, college counselor, and placement director. The key to success: publicize your services on campus radio and television, in the campus newspaper, on the bulletin boards, in dormitory bull sessions, in the fraternity, over a cup of coffee in the student center.

It is not that students dislike work; they just do not know much about the world of work. Similarly, it is not that students consciously avoid help in counseling and placement, they just do not realize it is there or cannot bring themselves to start what they suspect may be a painful and uncertain process.

Principle 9—A major purpose of career counseling is to help the student help himself.

The motivation of students is indeed an art. It may take the form of advisement about a summer job; it may arouse the curiosity of the student about himself so that he wants some objective psychological measurements taken; it may lead to counseling and the taking of a hard look at himself, his values, and goals. Whatever techniques used by the counselor, they must motivate the student to help himself.

Implications of Principle 9—The placement educator cannot make students' decisions—and he must not. The counselor's role is that of motivating the student to evaluate himself, his educational and vocational direction in the light of the opportunities which surround him. Perhaps the most difficult motivational task of all is to get the counselee to initiate a course of action consonant with his self-evaluation.

As the reader reflects on the basic assumptions set forth in this chapter, he should bear in mind that the greatest criticism of the career counselor, vocational counselor, placement director—title him as you will—is leveled at his lack of guiding principles in counseling and placement in keeping with recent studies, research, and learning.

The principles in this chapter have been suggested primarily to stimulate the imagination of the reader. Every placement educator is urged to develop his own set of principles and practices consistent with the most recent research in the behavioral sciences. Principles and practices will vary with the purposes and personality of the institution.

BIBLIOGRAPHY

1 Gesell, Arnold, et al., *Gesell Developmental Schedules*, The Psychological Corporation, New York, 1949.

2 Flavell, J. H., *The Developmental Psychology of Jean Piaget*, D. Van Nostrand Co., Inc., New Jersey, 1963.

3 Super, D. E., and Bachrach, P. B., *Scientific Careers and Vocational Development Theory*, Columbia University Teachers College Bureau of Publications, New York, 1957.

CHAPTER 4

Placement Office Services

T HE OFFICE OF CAREER COUNSELING, guided by educationally sound principles and practices, can play a major role
in the development of the college student. The degree of success which the placement office enjoys will depend on how well
it is accepted by its constituencies. Acceptance does not come
easily; it must be earned. Furthermore, no matter how good the
service, it may not be used unless it is well publicized. Placement, through its variety of student services, is in an ideal position to help students help themselves.

Freshman Orientation

The placement office has a responsibility to students to aid
them in reality orientation. On some campuses the course content, what goes on in the classroom, the counsel received from
faculty, seldom touch base with life. Some college placement
offices have, therefore, sought early to establish rapport with the
student body. A spot on the freshman orientation program can
usually be had for the asking.

Given an opportunity to speak, highly successful recent graduates with enthusiasm for alma mater and with unusual ability to communicate, will help both to bring the student face to face with the real world of work and, at the same time, to sell the placement office to the freshmen. Top-notch graduates will be happy to come back to campus to discuss such subjects as "What I Wish They Had Told Me As a Freshman," or "If I Had It To Do Over Again," or "Someday You're Going To Go To Work—Start Planning Now."

During freshman week a pamphlet or mimeographed materials describing career counseling services should get into the hands of all freshmen. In the small college, the placement director has the unusual opportunity to meet and be met by students on this occasion. Perhaps this is the moment to register students for part-time jobs.

Student Employment: Part-time and Summer

Certainly one of the first responsibilities of the placement office is to help provide financial assistance to needy students by making available part-time job opportunities both on and off campus through local employers. The placement office that is doing its job best will use the student employment situation as a means of occupational development; advisement and guidance will focus the student's attention on his value goals, what he expects to get out of a part-time job in addition to needed funds, and how that job may be of vocational significance.

It becomes, then, a necessity of placement to reach out into both the campus community and the community at large in order to maintain contacts with a variety of employers that can offer part-time employment. The telephone, personal letters, the newspaper, radio, and television can be helpful. Of course the person in charge of this program should know, on a first-hand basis, as many as possible of the employers with whom he is dealing; hence, this means personal visitation at times when the work load is not as heavy.

Once a flow of part-time jobs is established, job listings, direct referrals, and personal contacts with employers can be arranged for students.

Summer employment can be an important factor in the development of the individual. The trouble is that significant summer employment is hard to come by. A very few companies make available a very few jobs for a very few top-notch students.

Each year, however, more businesses make available significant work experiences for the college student. For example, a pharmaceutical company develops summer programs of employment for a limited number of students. "Each program involves a specially designed project concerning a current corporate problem . . . projects range from financial planning and analysis to analysis and evaluation of package design to studying the action of chemicals on enzymes and drug metabolism." [1]

Several insurance companies have developed summer internship programs in which internees are assigned to significant work projects. Likewise a few banks have developed on-the-job summer projects which expose the summer employee to the full scope of the bank's functions through work, lectures, conferences, and seminars. At a New York bank summer work projects have included such tasks as analyzing the results of the bank's long-range forecast, analyzing potential new overseas locations, the study and analysis of the credit worthiness of receivables held by large borrowing customers.[2]

Many more such opportunities, if created by business, would go a long way to developing a better understanding of business by college youth.

There are, also, a few worthwhile programs of summer work at both state and national levels of government and in a few non-profit organizations, including education.

There is no substitute for work experience in helping the individual to develop vocational and value goals. There is potential value in almost any summer job—camp, waitress, sales, or what have you. Such employment can give the individual a sense of his own strengths and limitations, a knowledge of how to deal with people, the discipline of a work situation, as well as valuable contact with reality. Every placement office should make considerable effort to aid students in securing both part-time and summer employment.

Financial Aid

A number of placement offices also direct the student financial aid program. There are both serious disadvantages and significant advantages to such a plan. One of the serious disadvantages is the dissipation of the energies of the staff in financial aid activities, leaving inadequate time for counseling and placement. On the other hand, dealing with students in financial aid matters does open the door to the placement office for the student, which in turn gives the placement office yet another chance to serve. Whether or not placement directs financial aid, the office will undoubtedly relate indirectly to financial aid since most aid packages these days are a combination of scholarship, loan, and part-time employment.

Occupational Information

One of the main thrusts of many college placement offices over the years has been the collecting and the giving of occupational information. What has often been overlooked in the past is that a student's receptivity to the occupational information available is conditioned by the feelings, attitudes, and perceptions he has already acquired from birth to college. Of occupational information Barry and Wolf have this to say:

> ". . . the child internalizes the information (beginning very early in life) in terms of his own perceptions and experiential background . . ." and this process "continues throughout a person's lifetime. The mental picture of what a secretary, a

doctor, an insurance salesman, or a banker does arises out of a person's perceptions of his experiences with these people. The person living in a small town envisions the banker either as the teller with whom he deals or as the financial tycoon he sees portrayed on television. From the information most meaningful to him, each individual creates his picture, erroneous or not, of the worker and the occupation. His concept of training, salary, duties, way of life, and working conditions arises out of this composite of information, experience, misinformation, wish fulfillment, and fantasy." [3]

Hence, the occupational information available to a student becomes significant in terms of where he is in his own vocational development at the time he uses the occupational information. This fact of life again emphasizes the importance of adequate counseling and guidance as precursors to effective use of the placement office's occupational information library. It also emphasizes the need to develop objective vocational understandings and attitudes beginning at the elementary school level.

Hoppock in a discussion of "What the Client Should Know About Occupations" [4] suggests that occupational information sources in placement offices should make it possible for students to become informed about: (1) employment prospects; (2) nature of work in an occupation; (3) work environment; (4) job qualifications; (5) unions; (6) discrimination; (7) preparation needed; (8) entrance job requirements; (9) advancement on the job; (10) earnings; (11) number and distribution of workers in various occupations; (12) advantages and disadvantages of particular employment.

Such information is found in a variety of sources: directories, encyclopedias, occupational brochures, company brochures, film strips, motion pictures, periodicals, etc. A full discussion of occupational information and the setting up of the vocational library is found in Chapter 6.

Education for Career Development

Perhaps, because the average placement office is understaffed, it never quite gets around to doing the many things that it might do to educate its various constituencies. For example, a regular feature column in the campus paper could show students how alumni progress in the world of work; it could show the paths of progress of alumni employed by recruiters currently on campus; it could relate research to company growth and the probable impact on the job market; it could feature whole new and little-known career areas brought about, for example, by space research. The opportunities here to educate are endless. Similar programs might be developed with the campus television and radio stations.

A display area in the library or student center, changed weekly, can serve as an important means of educating and motivating. Classroom learning could be supplemented by mimeographed materials quoting from a wide array of periodicals on the world of work which, in particular, relate education to work. A constant flow of materials (clippings, company reports, brochures, research findings, etc.) to department heads from placement can help serve several purposes: public relations for placement, education for the faculty, and bridging of the gap between academia and placement.

A great variety of other educational services can be developed, such as the supplying of employer contacts helpful to the professor preparing specific research, class demonstrations, or lecture work.

Student organizations are forever casting about for speakers. Several placement offices have been responsible for their college commencement speakers—board chairmen and company presidents available to their colleges because placement directors maintained fruitful company contacts.

The Careers Conference

Careers conferences have had cycles of popularity ever since 1913 when the careers conferences for women convened at the University of Wisconsin.[5] In time of recession the numbers in attendance are greater; in periods of affluence the attendance drops. No matter at what point in the cycle, occupational information brought to campus through speakers and panels representing a variety of occupations can have sound educational value. Student involvement in planning and executing the conference will help assure a greater success for such a program. Fraternities and clubs might sponsor various parts of, or all of the conference.

Alumni who are not too ancient, yet who have had successful careers, who have the ability to establish an easy rapport with the younger generation, and above all alumni who are enthusiastic and good speakers, can help make the careers conference succeed. No one should be invited to speak unless his capabilities are known!

How the careers program develops is of little consequence. It could be an evening event, an all-day program, a program run an hour a week over a number of weeks, or a program decentralized through various clubs and fraternities. The average placement officer can dream up a hundred and one ways to make a successful program. It is important to be sure that the program is well conceived and well publicized, and that those invited to speak can indeed speak!

Career Counseling

The most important student service of all is career counseling. It is the responsibility of placement—through education, counseling, guidance, and advisement—to make students aware of their own potential and how that potential may be used productively in the world of work. Counseling must begin with the student early enough in order to give time for the creation of an environment conducive to vocational development and growth. The senior year is not early enough. The sooner after one enters college that such counseling and guidance can begin, the better.

Much has been said in previous chapters about counseling and guidance. Let it here be stated simply that it is a responsibility of placement to make resources available that will encourage career exploration: counselors or a referral system to counseling; guidance materials such as handbooks, brochures, placement publications, the occupational library; psychological testing services; part-time employment in which to explore counseling findings; guidance to aid in the search for and evaluation of career choice, company selection, etc. Alumni, it has been found, are invaluable in advisement.

Personnel Files

The developing and maintaining of student and alumni personnel files is an important service of placement. Just what to include in such files is a difficult question to resolve. (See Appendix for special form.) Among the information such files might contain are: (1) registration forms, (2) records of interviews, (3) psychological test results, (4) transcripts of grades, (5) recommendations of part-time and summer employers, (6) faculty appraisals, (7) certain anecdotal information, as well as (8) recommendations of permanent full-time employers. In developing and maintaining the personnel file, confidentiality must be enforced (see Chapter 10). Whether it be mechanical or manual, some system must be developed for classification and rapid identification of students and alumni according to college major, job experience, job preferences.

Employer Files

In a similar fashion, records on transactions with employers must be maintained. Identification data on each employer should be developed to include such basic information as type of employer, subsidiaries, employer services and/or products, job descriptions, qualifications sought in candidates, salary details, summer employment, etc. Where job offers are accepted, some system will need to be developed to record the progress of the alumnus within the company.

The maintenance of up-to-date files is an invaluable service to students, alumni, and employers.

Services to Alumni

Most placement offices will want to serve their alumni. However, the novice in placement should be warned that alumni placement cannot just be "piggy-backed" on senior placement with any kind of effective results. Several factors unrelated to senior placement confront the alumni placement officer. To begin with, the alumni will present widely varying ranges of experience. A search, therefore, may often be necessary to find employers looking for candidates with particular experiences. While the graduating senior may be flexible in terms of geographic location, the alumnus may have sunk his roots deeply into a community and, therefore, have become inflexible geographically. Some placement offices have tried using the alumni bulletin as a vehicle to communicate employer jobs available, but the time lag from receipt of notice of job openings to the date of publication of bulletin is usually so great as to make this approach of questionable value.

Some colleges mail lists of job openings to alumni seeking placement assistance; others have tried mass mailings of alumni résumés to employers. Occasionally, this approach has resulted in an alumnus losing his job because his employer found he was job-hunting. Alumni listings, too, are difficult to keep current with employers.

One extremely serious problem which arises with many placement directors in dealing with alumni is an ethical one. The placement director may know of excellent job openings; he may know, too, of an alumnus happily employed whom he believes could well fill the job. Will he stir discontent in the alumnus by notifying him of the opening? Will he risk the ire of the employer by perhaps causing him to lose a good employee? These are serious problems to be considered in the alumni-placement-employer relationship (see Chapter 10).

The placement office, through the College Placement Council, makes available to graduates the Graduate Résumé Accumulation and Distribution (GRAD) System. This is a computerized means of matching the qualifications of college alumni with company job specifications. This system is designed to give employers throughout the country a chance to locate college graduates. It serves all types of disciplines, including engineering, science, liberal arts, business, and finance.

Some placement offices maintain a relationship with a few reliable commercial employment agencies. A new breed of employment agency was created several years ago, often started by former recruiters or placement officers, and operated under the title of manpower consultant or personnel consultant. Some agencies are to be recommended to alumni; others are to be carefully avoided. The placement director, from his own experience, can determine which might be of help to the alumni of his institution.

Experimentation with various techniques of job solicitation, alumni notification, how best to relate employers to alumni, and how to resolve the time-lag problem, are worthy of the efforts expended by placement. It goes without saying that alumni are an important part of any college; they are a major factor in both the moral and financial support of a college. Therefore, the more effectively a college can serve its alumni, the better it is for the college.

Follow-up

Continuing follow-up of alumni has great value to any college. It would appear that there might be two approaches to follow-up—one via the employer, the other via the alumnus. Employer participation has been sought by a number of colleges in follow-up studies. However, because employers respect the confidentiality of an employee's record, little information of consequence is made available to the college after the first several years of employment. Follow-up, therefore, will depend upon the cooperation of the alumni.

Some offices of career counseling do annual follow-up studies of the 5-, 10-, and 15-year classes (see Appendix). In addition, many do more comprehensive studies periodically in connection with gathering data for alumni directories (see Appendix—for directory questionnaire). The findings of such studies can be useful to the counselor in developing case studies; sometimes the findings may motivate curriculum changes or help to improve procedures in placement.

Since the purposes of alumni follow-up will vary from college to college, the type of data secured, together with the methods of accumulating the information, will vary. The burden of extra work created in follow-up is small indeed compared with the value received through the channels of communication which are opened with alumni.

Services to Employers

Through the services of the placement office, the college and the employer operate a mutual assistance program. The college and the employer need to cultivate one another to the point of establishing productive working relationships. With this in mind, placement personnel should attempt to visit a substantial number of prospective employers annually: business establishments, government and social agencies, departments of education, scientific and research centers, etc. Two factors usually determine visits to employers: the kinds of employment for which graduating seniors and alumni search and for which they are qualified, and geographical preference in location.

The list of employer prospects is never complete. It needs to be updated constantly, removing from the list employers with whom contacts have been unproductive and adding to the list newly established contacts. Obviously, it is "results" for the employer that will keep him coming, but the student must always be put first. Will this job give him the opportunity to use his abilities? Is the location congenial? What has been the previous experience of alumni with the employer?

Services to the employer generally include notifying candidates of particular employment openings, background information on candidates, arrangements to interview candidates, provision of interview space on campus or arrangements with candidates for interviews on the employers' premises. In addition, in order to facilitate the employer-candidate interview, but even more to make available occupational information, a library of employer brochures is maintained. Candidates are expected to make themselves knowledgeable about employers in advance of interviews. It is important that the employer brochure library be updated annually.

Research

The average placement director is sitting on piles of accumulated raw data which, if studied, analyzed, and reported out, might be of value both to students and employers. As an example, placement offices probably have more information collecting dust than any other single source on factors that influence vocational choice: the relationship between grades, job choice and career development; part-time jobs and how they affect career choice, etc. For their own good and the good of their profession, they need to get the results of studies of these data out into the main stream.

Public Relations

Some interesting by-products are available from studies done by Stephens and Stevens on student attitudes toward employment.[6] They found that the placement office which has the best image with the students is the one that works hard at doing those things that make for a good image, and then tells the students over and over again in a variety of ways what it is doing. Such placement offices know the power of communication; they tell their story to the students via campus radio, television, and newspaper; they tell it to faculty and staff via bulletins, bulletin boards, and luncheons; they tell it to the alumni in the alumni bulletin, and their story gets to the trustees in the annual report.

It is not what the facts in any situation are but what people think they are. An aggressive public relations program helps to narrow the gap between the facts and what people think they are.

BIBLIOGRAPHY

1 "Seeking a Summer Challenge?," recruitment brochure, Eli Lilly and Co.

2 "Recruiting Nationwide for Summer Employment Positions," First National City Bank of New York.

3 Barry, Ruth and Wolf, Beverly, *An Epitaph for Vocational Guidance,* Bureau of Publications, Teachers College, Columbia University, New York 1962, pp. 76–77.

4 Hoppock, Robert, *Occupational Information,* McGraw-Hill Book Co., Inc., New York, pp. 17–27.

5 Chervenik, Emily, "Thirty-five Years of Careers Conferences," *Journal of National Association of Deans of Women,* March 1948, pp. 145–148.

6 Stephens, Everett W. and Stevens, Nancy, "What Motivates Vocational Choice?," an unpublished paper presented at the annual convention of the American Personnel and Guidance Association, Dallas, Texas, 1966.

CHAPTER 5

Organization and Facility Patterns

A N EFFECTIVE PLACEMENT ORGANIZATIONAL pattern is one in which the director of placement reports directly to the dean of students, who, in turn, reports to the vice president for student affairs. In some of the smaller colleges, placement personnel may report directly to the president, thus bypassing the dean. While this may offer a line of communication directly to the top, such organization may well create problems because communication tends to be short-circuited with the dean of students. Direct contact with the dean, while it cannot guarantee a necessary relationship with counseling services, may help develop essential liaison, the importance of which has been discussed in earlier chapters. Hopefully the day will come soon when counseling and placement functions will come under one roof closely integrated in the best interest of the student.

Within placement itself two basic patterns prevail: centralized and decentralized placement offices. In the opinion of most, the centralized office is more effective, more efficient, and more economical to operate than the decentralized office. Proponents of the decentralized office argue that a decentralized office is more personal, less mechanical, and, therefore, more effective in dealing with students as individuals.

The Centralized Office

A centralized pattern is found in most institutions of higher learning today. In centralized placement all the placement staff, activities, and essential accouterments are centralized in one office: career counseling and guidance activities, graduate school catalogues, occupational information, and employer literature; current employment market information, vocational tests, and student records.

Within the large college and university, the staff is usually organized by function: career counseling and guidance, guidance on graduate work, part-time employment, summer employment, full-time employment, alumni employment. In the larger placement operations, full-time employment activities may be further divided among specialists in teacher placement, placement of engineers, liberal arts and business students, graduate placement, etc. A variety of effective patterns can emerge.

The Decentralized Office

The functions of decentralized placement are similar to those of the centralized office except that they are not centrally directed; placement is fragmented either by function or by geographical location, or perhaps by a combination of both factors. For example, in a large university the schools of engineering and education may stand side by side. There probably was a time in their development when each was more an independent entity than the coordinate part of the university that it is today. During those days of greater separateness, many colleges within their university framework developed separate placement offices. Some of the oldest placement offices still continue as decentralized operations. The engineering school may remain separated in placement activity because, it is argued, in many ways teacher and engineering placement require quite different approaches to employment. This argument, while on the surface appearing logical, is perhaps overworked and not too consistent. Engineering students as well as education students require counsel and guidance; they refer to occupational and employer libraries; records have to be kept on them.

Some universities, because of their scattered facilities throughout a metropolitan area, have developed decentralized offices. This is unfortunate, for one centralized office can avoid duplications in libraries, record-keeping, physical space; even more important, the centralized office can pool all of its greater resources for the benefit of any student. As to the argument that the decentralized office is more friendly, one can only say that friendliness is not unique to decentralization. Employers, generally, are not too happy with decentralization; the opportunity to make their needs known once at the university and then to have the total resources of the university go to work for them, makes for more effective recruiting.

The late Paul Boynton of Standard Oil, a recruiter who made considerable impact upon recruitment and placement during his lifetime, had this to say:

> "Too much time and effort, as well as expense, are wasted for the college, the students, and the employer when it is necessary for the recruiter to engage with as many as a half-dozen separate department heads in one school . . . the writer feels it unadvisable to visit many schools which do not centralize personnel and placement activities . . ." [1]

Norman Hillis has similar comments:

> "Without a central placement office the employer is found with a tremendous problem . . ." [2]

Robert Calvert, Jr., in his thesis on "A College Placement Program," sums up his findings this way:

"With a centralized office, employer, students, and faculty members know where to turn for placement information and assistance . . ." [3]

Likewise, one office, which serves the needs of a student who may wish to cross functional lines, can offer the student a more comprehensive service. Finally, the centralized office generally reflects an all-college or all-university concern that placement is an integral part of the total educational process.

Personnel Requirements

In the small college one or two staff members, together with supporting clerical workers, may do all placement work, including counseling and guidance. It is held by some that the staff worker who is charged with across-the-board responsibilities—one who counsels his clients as well as works with them in job-hunting—should be a more perceptive counselor.

There is no magic ratio of counselors to students; here, again, it depends upon how the counselor relates to the student. For example, the part-time employment operation is relatively simple. Extensive counseling is probably not necessary; some guidance may be helpful; the relationship for the most part is often that of advising. In such a setting, a ratio of 350 active student registrants to one professional counselor, with supporting clerical help, may be quite adequate. However, in matters of counseling in graduate school or career employment, the ratio would need to be lowered considerably to a 100–1 ratio, or thereabouts (active registrants to professional counselors, and supporting staff).

The more an office can mechanize, in terms of collecting, storing, and retrieving information on students and employers, either through direct access to a computer, or on-line computer services, the more time there will be left for the essential work of counseling.

Facilities

The folklore in placement is replete with stories (and herein truth is stranger than fiction) about the ways in which placement has been relegated to facilities in the clock tower which no one wanted but the bats, or hidden away in some basement area shared by the rats. There can be little doubt that the type of physical facility assigned to placement is in fairly direct ratio to the importance it is given in the eyes of the administration; placement directors need to be able to "sell" their services.

If the director is lucky enough to be able to select the location for the placement office, one criterion should be kept in mind—students. Locate the office at the crossroads, where the student traffic is, wherever that may be. Today, on most campuses, a high traffic count can be made at the student center.

The ideal arrangement would be a block of space within the suite of the dean of students, adjacent to counseling services and next to the registrar's office. Such an arrangement would both enhance communication with other student personnel services and, having close proximity to the registrar's office, could make it unnecessary to duplicate certain records.

How much space does a placement center need? This, again, depends upon how specialized or how comprehensive the placement activities are in relation to the size of the student body. (See Appendix for some sample floor plans.)

The office of the dean may range from 400–600 square feet; the offices of the directors of placement and counseling might range from 300–500 square feet with assistants' space averaging 225–250 square feet. Testing and interviewing cubicles need not be large, approximately 75 square feet, but it is absolutely essential that they be soundproof, well lighted, and well ventilated. One problem with interview-cubicle-space is that during half the college year there is never enough space; during the other half, the interview rooms lie idle. The number of cubicles needed will depend on the degree of testing and counseling taking place, plus the number of employers recruiting, and the placement office's ability to make maximum use of space in scheduling. In a student body of 2,500–3,000, a combination reception-library area ought to range from 750–1,000 square feet. Secretarial-clerical space again is dependent upon size of staff which in turn is dependent upon the degree of service rendered.

An 80-square-foot space is generally recommended for each secretarial-clerical employee, using a 60-inch desk, chair, one file, and a visitor's chair. Fifty-square-foot averages are considered adequate for clerical workers.[4]

It goes without saying that the décor of the office helps to entice students as well as to give the recruiter a particular impression about the institution.

A problem of any library is to get the books out where they will be used. Keep in mind that the placement office has three types of materials to display: give-away, loan, and reference. The give-aways will be primarily employer literature. This material should be placed for "impulse" pick-up. Other materials need to be in a supervised check-out area. If space arrangements permit, an ideal location for the library is between the counseling and placement facilities.

A variety of display techniques can be utilized. They range from table displays, to shelf compartments, to the magazine type of rack display, to the file cabinet. Which type best fits the college needs, décor, and budget?

There should be adequate arrangement in space to provide effective accommodations for reception, student registration and interview sign-up, testing and interviewing, as well as areas designated for the occupational information center, display of company brochures, group meetings and conferences, in addition to the usual filing space needed.

BIBLIOGRAPHY

1 Boynton, Paul W., "Recruiting for Industry," *School and College Placement,* October 1940, pp. 31–33.

2 Hillis, Norman D., "Wanted: A Blueprint for a College Placement Office," *School and College Placement,* Dec. 1950, p. 44.

3 Calvert, Robert Jr., "A College Placement Program," Doctoral Thesis, p. 35.

4 Robichaud, Beryl, *Selecting, Planning and Managing Office Space,* McGraw-Hill Book Co., New York, 1958, pp. 83 ff.

CHAPTER 6

Occupational Information and the Vocational Library

ONE OF THE ESSENTIAL TASKS of the placement office is to gather information about occupations and to develop a vocational library. Career literature must be organized in a well-ordered, logical fashion. And because occupational opportunities are in constant flux, an occupational information library is very dynamic. Some experts recommend an annual burning to insure that obsolete information is cleared regularly from the files!

Much of the material which follows in this chapter is adapted from "The Career Information Collection for Colleges and Universities," a publication project of the Eastern College Personnel Officers. Permission to use these materials was granted by that association. Project committee members of the Eastern College Personnel Officers whose work is hereby acknowledged are:

Stanley N. Kinney, *Chairman*
Alva C. Cooper
Lenore Pockman
Julia E. Read
Robert Hoppock

Developing a Filing System

Several ready-made filing systems are available to the placement office just commencing an occupational information library:

1. Science Research Associates Career Information Kit Filing System. This system is based on the arrangement of job titles found in the *Dictionary of Occupational Titles.*
2. Bennett Occupational Filing Plan. This is an alphabetical subject index by fields of work based upon the *Dictionary of Occupational Titles.*
3. Chronicle Plan for Filing Occupational Information. This system, too, is based on the *Dictionary of Occupational Titles.*

Actually each placement office should develop its own filing system designed specifically to meet the needs of the particular college, its curricula, and the types of employment its graduates generally seek. A sample system such as that which might be devised for a coeducational, liberal arts college follows:

Suggested Headings for a Career Literature File

ARCHITECTURE
ARMED FORCES
—General
—Men
—Women
ART
—General
—Acting, Dancing, etc.
—Cartooning
—Commercial Design
—Creative Art
—Fashion Design

—Interior Decorating
—Music
—Photography
BUSINESS
—Accounting
—Advertising
—Computer Control, Planning, and Programming
—Construction and Development
—Entrepreneur
—Finance

—Import-Export
—Industrial Relations
—Management
—Manufacturing
—Marketing-Sales
—Personnel
—Research
—Secretarial-Clerical
—Transportation
ECOLOGY
EDITING AND PUBLISHING
EDUCATION
—General
—Library Work
—Museum Work
—Teaching: General
—Teaching: College
—Teaching: Elementary School
—Teaching: Home Economics
—Teaching: Kindergarten and
  Nursery School
—Teaching: Physical Educa-
  tion
—Teaching: Secondary
ENGINEERING
—Aerospace
—Automotive
—Chemicals
—Electronics
—Iron and Steel
—Petroleum
—Textiles
—Utilities
FOREIGN LANGUAGES
GOVERNMENT
—General
—Federal
—Federal Abroad
—Municipal
—State
HEALTH
—General
—Chiropody
—Dentistry and Related Fields
—Food Service

—Laboratory and Medical
  Technology
✕Medical Illustration
—Medical Library Work
—Medical Secretarial Careers
—Medicine: Physicians and
  Surgeons
—Nursing
—Optometry and Related
  Fields
—Osteopathic Medicine
—Pharmacy
—Podiatry
—Psychiatry
—Public Health
—Red Cross
—Therapy: Physical, Occupa-
  tional, etc.
—Veterinary Medicine
HOME ECONOMICS
LAW
MATHEMATICS
—Data Processing
—Programming
—Research
—Statistics
MISCELLANEOUS
PSYCHOLOGY
PUBLIC RELATIONS
RECREATION
RELIGION
RESEARCH
SCIENCE, LIFE
—General
—Agronomy and Forestry
—Botany, Horticulture
—Microbiology
—Pathology
—Physiology
SCIENCE, PHYSICAL
—General
—Astronomy
—Biochemistry
—Cartography
—Chemistry

—Geology and Geophysics
—Meteorology
—Mineralogy
—Oceanography
—Physics
SOCIAL SCIENCES
—General
—Archeology and Anthropology

—Economics
—Geography
—Social Work
VACATION AND PART-TIME WORK
WRITING
—General
—Journalism
—Technical

A Suggested Cross Index to Occupations

Occupation	*Field Under*
Accountant	Business
Actor, Actress	Art: Creative Art—Dramatic Artist
Actuary	Business
Administrator, Business	Business: Management
Administrator, Hospital	Business: Management
Administrator, Personnel	Business: Management
Administrator, Public and Government, Federal, State, City	Government: Management
Administrator, School	Education: Management
Advertising Artist	Advertising
Advertising Copy Writer	Advertising
Aeronautical Engineer	Engineering: Structural
Aerospace Engineer	Aeronautical Engineering
Agricultural Research Specialist	Research: Agriculture
Agricultural Specialist	Science: Life Sciences
Air Force	Armed Forces: Air Force
Airlines	Aerospace Industry
Anesthetist	Health Careers
Animal Husbandman	Science: Life Sciences
Announcer	Television and Radio
Anthropologist	Social Sciences
Archeologist	Social Sciences
Architect	Art: Creative Art
Architectural Engineer	Engineering: Structural
Archivist	Library Science
Armed Forces	Government
Army	Armed Forces: Army
Army Aviator	Armed Forces: Army
Army Special Service Worker	Government: Federal

Occupation	*Field Under*
Artist, Advertising	Art: Graphic Arts
Astronomer	Sciences: Physical Sciences
Athlete	Recreation Leadership
Athletic Coach	Recreation Leadership
Atomic Scientist	Science: Physical and Nuclear Sciences
Attorney	Law
Audiologist	Health Careers: Speech Therapist and Audiologist
Auditor	Business: Accounting
Author	Writing
Automotive Engineer	Engineering: Mechanical
Aviator	Aerospace Industry
Bacteriologist	Science: Life Sciences
Banker	Business: Banking
Bilingual Secretary	Linguist: See also secretary
Biochemist	Science: Physical Sciences
Biologist	Science: Life Science
Botanist	Science: Life Sciences
Buyer	Business: Sales
Cartographer	Science: Physical Sciences
Cartoonist	Art: Commercial Art
Cashier	Business: Accounting
Ceramic Engineer	Engineering: Industrial
Certified Public Accountant	Business: Accounting
Chaplain	Religion
Chef	Home Economics: Food and Nutrition
Chemist	Science: Physical Sciences
Chemical Engineer	Engineering: Industrial
Chemical Research Specialist	Research: Chemistry
Chiropodist	Health
Chiropractor	Health
Choreographer	Art: **Creative** Art—Dancing and Choreography
City Manager	Government: Municipal
City Planner	Government: Municipal
Civil Engineer	Engineering: Structural
Clerical Worker, Civil Service	Government: Federal
Coast Guard	Armed Forces: Coast Guard
Commercial Designer	Art: Commercial Design
Communications Engineer	Engineering: Electrical and Nuclear

Occupation	Field Under
Communications Technician	Engineering: Electrical and Nuclear
Composer	Art: Creative Art—Music
Comptroller	Business: Accounting
Conductor, Musical	Art: Creative Art—Music
Conservationist	Science: Life Sciences
Construction	Business: Construction and Development (See also Civil Engineering)
Consumer Relations	Public Relations
Corporation Lawyer	Law
Cost Accountant	Business: Accounting
Counselor, Camp	Recreation Leadership
Court Reporter	Business: Secretarial and Clerical
Criminologist	Government: Federal
Critic	Writing
Dancer	Art: Creative Art
Dental Assistant	Health
Dental Hygienist	Health
Dental Laboratory Technician	Health
Dental Surgeon	Health
Dentist	Health
Designer	Art: Commercial Design
Diesel Engineer	Engineering: Mechanical
Dietitian	Home Economics: Nutrition and Dietetics
Diplomatic Service	Government: Federal
Director of Religious Education	Religion
Draftsman	Engineering: Structural
Dramatic Artist	Art: Creative Art
Ecologist	Ecology
Economic Research	Business: Research
Economist	Social Sciences
Editor	Writing
Electrical Engineer	Engineering: Electrical and Nuclear
Electronics Engineer	Engineering: Electrical and Nuclear
Entomologist	Science: Life Sciences
Entrepreneur	Business: Management
Export	Business: Sales
Farm Equipment	Business: Sales
F.B.I.	Government: Federal—Department of Justice

Occupation	*Field Under*
* Federal Civil Service	Government: Federal
Fish and Wildlife Service	Government: Federal
Food Chemist	Home Economics: Food and Nutrition
Food Processing Research	Home Economics: Food and Nutrition
Food Service	Home Economics: Food and Nutrition
Food Technologist	Home Economics: Food and Nutrition
Foreign Commerce	Business: Import-Export
Foreign Service	Government: Federal
Forester	Science: Life Sciences
Free-Lance Writer	Writing
Geneticist	Science: Life Sciences
Geodesist	Science: Physical Sciences
Geographer	Science: Physical Sciences
Geologist	Science: Physical Sciences
Geophysicist	Science: Physical Sciences
Geriatrics	Science: Life Sciences
Guidance Counselor	Education: Guidance and Testing
Historian	Social Sciences
Home Economics Research	Home Economics
Home Economist	Home Economics
Home Management	Home Economics
Horticulturist	Science: Life Sciences
Hospital Plant Superintendent	Business: Management
Hotel Management	Home Economics: Food Service Administration
Housing and Redevelopment	Government: Municipal
Immigration	Government: Federal
Import, Export	Business: Import-Export
Industrial Engineer	Engineering: Industrial
Industrial Relations	Business: Industrial and Labor Relations
Insurance	Business: Finance
Internal Revenue	Government: Federal—Treasury Department
Interpreter	Linguist
Interpretive Reader	Art: Creative Art—Drama

* An alphabetical listing of federal civil service occupations may be found in the booklet *Federal Careers in the Sixties—A Guide for College Students* filed under "Government: Federal."

Occupation	Field Under
Inventor	Research
Investment Consultant	Business: Investments
Journalist	Writing
Laboratory Technician	Health
Labor Economist	Social Sciences: Economics
Labor Relations	Business: Industrial and Labor Relations
Landscape Architect	Agriculture
Lawyer	Law
Librarian	Education
Librarian, Government	Government: Federal
Marine Corps	Armed Forces: Marine Corps
Marine Engineer	Engineering: Mechanical
Marketing	Business: Marketing
Marketing Research	Business: Research
Mathematician	Mathematics: (See Data Processing, Programming, Research, Statistics)
Mechanical Engineering	Engineering: Mechanical
Medical Assistant	Health
Medical Doctor	Health
Medical Illustrator	Art: Illustration
Medical Physicist	Health
Medical Records Librarian	Health
Medical Research Specialist	Research: Medicine
Medical Social Work	Social Sciences: Sociologist, Social Work
Merchandising	Business: Marketing
Merchant Marine	Transportation
Metallurgical Engineer	Engineering: Industrial
Meteorologist	Science: Physical Sciences
Microbiologist	Science: Life Sciences—Biology
Minerologist	Science: Physical Sciences
Minister	Religion
Missionary	Religion
Music Director: Religious	Music
Musician	Music
Navy	Armed Forces: Navy
News Commentator	Writing
Newspaper Reporter	Writing

Occupation	*Field Under*
Nurse, Registered, Hospital, Industrial	Health
Oceanographer	Science: Physical Sciences
Office Manager	Business: Management
Optician	Health
Optometrist	Health
Orthoptic Technician	Health
Osteopathic Physician	Health
Overseas Positions, Government	Government: Federal
Overseas Positions, Non-Government	Business—Education
Packaging Engineer	Engineering: Industrial
Parole and Probation Officer, Municipal	Government: Municipal
Parole and Probation Officer, State	Government: State; also see Municipal
Pathologist	Sciences: Life Sciences
Personnel	Business: Personnel
Patent Attorney	Law
Petroleum Engineer	Engineering: Industrial
Pharmacist (Retail, Hospital, and Manufacturing)	Health
Photogrammetrist	Science: Physical Sciences
Photographer	Art: Commercial
Photo-Journalist	Writing
Physical Education	Recreation
Physician	Health
Physicist	Science: Life Sciences
Physiologist	Science: Life Sciences
Playground Director	Recreation
Playwright	Writing
Podiatrist	Health
Political Scientist	Social Sciences
Portrait Photographer	Art: Commercial Art
Press Agent	Public Relations
Priest	Religion
Probation and Parole Officer	Government: Municipal, State
Producer (Theatrical Productions)	Art: Theater
Professional Association Director	Public Relations
Programmer	Mathematics

Occupation	*Field Under*
Psychiatric Nurse	Health
Psychiatric Social Worker	Social Sciences: Sociology, Psychiatry
Psychiatrist	Psychology and Health
Psychologist	Psychology
Public Health Educator	Education: See Health
Public Health Physician	Health
Public Opinions Analyst	Public Relations
Publicity Worker	Public Relations
Public Relations Specialist	Public Relations
Publishing and Printing	Business: Service
Rabbi	Religion
Radio Engineer	Engineering: Electrical
Radio Writer	Writing: Television and Radio
Real Estate Agent, Broker	Business: Marketing
Real Estate	Business: Management
Receptionist	Business: Personnel
Recreation	Recreation Leadership
Religious Social Worker	Social Work—Religion
Research Scientist	Research: Science
Restaurant Manager	Home Economics: Food Service Administration
Retailing	Business: Marketing
Safety Engineer	Engineering: Industrial
Salesman	Business: Marketing
Sanitation	Health
School Administrator	Education
Scientist	Science
Sculptor	Art: Creative Art
Secretary	Business: Secretarial—Clerical
Secret Service Work	Government: Federal
Singer	Art: Music
Social Science Researcher	Research: Social Sciences
Social Security Work	Government: Federal—Department of Health, Education, and Welfare
Social Work	Social Sciences: Sociologist, Social Work
Sociologist	Social Sciences
Soil	Science: Life Sciences

Occupation	*Field Under*
S.P.A.R.	Armed Forces: Coast Guard; also see Army
Stage Manager	Art: Theater
State Department Work	Government: Federal
Statistician	Mathematics
Stenographer	Business: Secretarial—Clerical
Stock Broker	Business: Investments
Summer Job Opportunities	Miscellaneous
Surgeon	Health
Surveyor	Engineering: Structural
Tax Accountant	Business: Accounting
Tax Lawyer	Law
Teacher	Education—see level sought
Technical Writer	Writing
Television and Radio Performer	Television and Radio
Television Writer	Writing: Television and Radio
Textile, Clothing and Merchandising	Home Economics
Theater	Art-Creative Arts
Therapist, Music	Health—Music
Therapist, Occupational	Psychology
Therapist, Physical	Health
Therapist, Speech and Hearing	Health—Psychology—Education
Trade Associations Work	Public Relations
Traffic Manager	Business: Transportation
Translator	Foreign Languages
Transportation	Business: Transportation
Travel Agency	Business: Service
Treasury Enforcement	Government: Federal—Treasury Department
Trucking	Business: Transportation
Vacation Job Opportunities	Miscellaneous: Vacation and Part-Time Job Opportunities
Veterinarian	Health
Vocational Counselor	Psychology: Education
Vocational Rehabilitation Counselor	See Therapist: Occupational
WAC	Armed Forces: Army
WAF	Armed Forces: Air Force; also see Army

Occupation	*Field Under*
WAVE	Armed Forces: Navy; also see Army
Wholesaler	Business: Marketing
Writer	Writing
X-Ray Technician	Health
Youth Organization Work	Recreation
Zoologist	Science: Life Sciences

Almost any one of these categories can be subdivided. Take education or engineering as examples. Under education there might be such subheads as "College and University," "Elementary School," "Preschool," "Secondary School," etc. Or education might be categorized as "Teacher-Art," "Exceptional Child," "Foreign Languages," "Music," "Religion," "Speech," etc. In a similar fashion, engineering may be broken down into its various functional areas. The point is to develop a reasonable working index for the particular institution to be served.

Building the Career Information Library

Where does one start in building the library? How extensive need the library be? A suggested collection appears at the end of this chapter. The materials to be included in any collection depend upon curricula, student interests, and types of employment generally sought.

Catalogues and Announcements—It is advisable to set up a separate section within the library in which graduate school catalogues are filed alphabetically. Students also need information about scholarships, assistantships, and fellowships. Here the recommended method of filing is by study area rather than by university name.

Employer Brochures—Employer brochures provide specific job information within a particular organization. Companies recruiting on campus generally expect interviewees to have read the company brochure. The simplest method of filing such material is alphabetically by company or organization.

Audio-Visuals—With the incorporation of multi-media halls in new college construction for lectures and demonstrations, students are becoming accustomed, as part of the classroom experience, to a variety of communications techniques: video-tapes, closed circuit television, sound film strips, motion pictures, slides, and tapes. There are relatively few ready-made sound film strips, motion pictures, and tapes that the placement director will want for the placement library, and there is no one source. Materials are available from businesses, foundations, colleges and universities, government.

The Computer—The day is near when the student will be able to get occupational information directly from the computer. The placement office will be "on-line" to the computer on a time-sharing basis via terminals within the placement office. By learning the simple operation of programming pertinent questions about job opportunities, companies, locations, characteristics sought in candidates, etc., the student will be able to get an immediate print-out of the information sought from the computer.

The placement officer will want to keep a close watch over the variety of vocational materials available through new media for there are bound to be revolutionary developments within the next few years.

Books

ANDERSON, RUTH I. *Secretarial Careers.* New York: H. Z. Walck, 1961. $3.75.

ASHWORTH, JOHN. *Careers in Accounting.* New York: H. Z. Walck, 1963. $3.75.

BAER, MAX F., AND ROEBER, EDWARD C. *Occupational Information: The Dynamics of Its Nature and Use.* Revised. Chicago: Science Research Associates, 1964. $7.50. Includes some discussion of the world of work, sources, kinds, and evaluation of occupational information.

Beck, Bertram M. *Your Future in Social Work.* (Careers in Depth Series) New York: Richards Rosen Press, 1964. $2.95.

Bergenfeld, Leonard. *Civil Service Jobs for You with the City of New York.* Garden City: Doubleday, 1965. $1.95-paper.

Bernays, Edward L. *Your Future in Public Relations.* (Careers in Depth Series) New York: Richards Rosen Press. 1961. $2.95.

Blood, Jerome W. (ed.). *Optimum Use of Engineering Talent.* New York: American Management Association, 1961. $9.00.

Calvert, Robert, Jr., and Steele, John E. *Planning Your Career.* New York: McGraw-Hill, 1963. $3.75.

Carey, John L. *The C.P.A. Plans for the Future.* New York: American Institute of C.P.A.'s, 1965. $5.00.

Carroll, John M. *Careers and Opportunities in Electronics.* New York: Dutton, 1963. $3.95.

Chamberlain, Jo Hubbard. *Careers for Social Scientists.* New York: H. Z. Walck, 1961. $3.75.

Cooper, Joseph D. *A Woman's Guide to Part-Time Jobs.* Dolphin Books edition. Garden City: Doubleday, 1963. $1.25-paper. A useful resource for women seeking part-time work. Gives good suggestions on where and how to find the job.

Curtis, Robert E. *Your Future in Music.* (Careers in Depth Series) Richards Rosen Press, 1962. $2.95.

Fichter, Joseph Henry. *Religion as an Occupation.* Notre Dame, Indiana: University of Notre Dame Press, 1961. $6.50.

Fried, Eleanor L. *Is the Fashion Business Your Business?* New York: Fairchild, 1961. $4.50.

Gately, Olive (ed.). *Your Future in the Fashion World.* (Careers in Depth Series) New York: Richards Rosen Press, 1960. $2.95.

Glaser, Barney G. *Organizational Scientists: Their Professional Careers.* Indianapolis: Bobbs-Merrill, 1964. $1.95-paper.

GRUBER, EDWARD. *Résumés That Get Jobs: How to Write Your Best Résumé.* Arco Publishing Co., 1963. $2.00-paper.

HAMMEL, FAYE (ed.). *The Mademoiselle Career Girl's Guide to New York.* New York: The Dial Press, 1962. $4.95. Written for the girl coming to New York on her own. Provides job hunting tips as well as suggestions in regard to living arrangements, recreation, and shopping.

HARMON, CHARLOTTE. *How to Break into the Theater.* New York: Dial Press, 1961. $4.00.

HOLDEN, DONALD. *Art Career Guide.* New York: Watson-Guptill Publications, 1961. $5.75.

HOPPOCK, ROBERT. *Occupational Information.* Second edition. New York: McGraw-Hill, 1963. $8.50. Although written for the high school counselor, it is a useful reference for college. The suggestions in regard to the evaluation, selection, and uses of occupational literature provide helpful guidelines.

HUMPHREYVILLE, THERESA R. *Futures for Home Economists.* Englewood Cliffs, New Jersey: Prentice-Hall, 1963. $6.95.

KAPLAN, ALBERT A. *Careers in Department Store Merchandising.* New York: H. Z. Walck, 1962. $3.75.

KING, ALICE GORE. *Career Opportunities for Women in Business.* New York: E. P. Dutton, 1963. $4.50.

LAWTON, SHERMAN PAXTON. *The Modern Broadcaster: The Station Book.* New York: Harper & Sons, 1961. $6.00.

LERCH, JOHN H. *Careers in Broadcasting.* New York: Appleton-Century-Crofts, 1962. $3.95.

LEVENSTEIN, AARON. *Why People Work.* New York: Crowell-Collier Press, 1962. $3.95.

LEWIS, ADELE, AND BOBROFF, EDITH. *From College to Career.* Indianapolis: Bobbs-Merrill Company, 1963. $3.95.

LIVINGSTON, ROBERT T. AND WAITE, WILLIAM W. *The Manager's Job.* New York: Columbia University Press, 1960. $10.00.

LOCKLEAR, EDMOND. *Your Future in Accounting.* (Careers in Depth Series) New York: Richards Rosen Press, 1963. $2.95.

MARSHALL, AUSTIN. *How to Get a Better Job*. New York: Appleton-Century-Crofts, 1964. $5.95.

MOORE, ROBERT FOSTER. *Blue Print Your Career: a Guide to Success*. Harrisburg, Penn.: Stackpole & Heck, 1949.

NOURSE, ALAN EDWARD, AND HALLIDAY, ELEANORE. *So You Want to Be a Nurse*. New York: Harper & Row, 1961. $3.50; $.60-paper.

—— *So You Want to Be a Scientist*. New York: Harper & Row, 1960. $3.50.

NUTTER, CAROLYN F. *The Résumé Workbook*. Cranston, Rhode Island: Carroll Press, 1964. $2.75.

PARADIS, ADRIAN A. *The New Look in Banking*. New York: David McKay, 1961. $3.50.

PARIS, JEANNE. *Your Future as a Home Economist*. (Careers in Depth Series) New York: Richards Rosen Press, 1964. $2.95.

PERLMAN, HELEN. *So You Want to Be a Social Worker*. New York: Harper & Row, 1962. $3.27.

PLUMMER, GAIL. *The Business of Show Business*. New York: Harper & Row, 1961. $5.25.

POLLACK, PHILIP. *Careers and Opportunities in Chemistry*. New York: E. P. Dutton, 1960. $3.50.

—— *Careers and Opportunities in Physics*. New York: E. P. Dutton, 1961. $3.75.

—— *Careers and Opportunities in Science*. Revised. New York: E. P. Dutton, 1965. $3.95.

POPHAM, ESTELL L. *Opportunities in Office Occupations*. New York: Vocational Guidance Manuals, 1964. $1.45.

RICH, ALAN. *Careers and Opportunities in Music*. New York: E. P. Dutton, 1964. $4.50.

ROOD, ALLAN. *Job Strategy*. New York: McGraw-Hill, 1961. $5.95.

RUSHING, WILLIAM A. *The Psychiatric Professions*. Chapel Hill: University of North Carolina Press, 1964. $6.00.

SCOTT, GEORGE A. *Your Future in Retailing*. New York: Richards Rosen Press, 1960. $2.95.

SINGER, JULES B. *Your Future in Advertising.* New York: Richards Rosen Press, 1960. $2.95.

SMITH, RALPH JUDSON. *Engineering as a Career.* 2d edition. New York: McGraw-Hill, 1962. $5.95; $4.50-paper.

STEINBERG, J. LEONARD. *Guide to Careers through College Majors.* San Diego: Robert R. Knapp, 1964. $3.95.

STRAUSS, ANSELM L. *The Professional Scientist: a Study of American Chemists.* Chicago: Aldine Publishing Co., 1965. $6.00.

THOMSON, VIRGIL. *The State of Music.* 2d edition revised. New York: Vintage Press, 1962. $1.25.

VAUGHAN, DANA P. (ed.). *Art Professions in the U.S.* New York: The Cooper Union School of Art and Architecture, 1960. Good discussion of art careers including qualifications and job application procedures. Appendix includes lists of accredited schools of art.

WACHS, THEODORE, JR. *Careers in Research Science.* New York: H. Z. Walck, 1961. $3.75.

WILLIAMSON, MARGARET. *Social Worker: Artist and Scientist in Human Relations.* New York: Macmillan, 1964. $3.95.

WINTER, ELMER. *A Woman's Guide to Earning a Good Living.* New York: Simon and Schuster, 1961. $4.95. Written for women already working or for those who want to work. Presents some of the "how-to-do" information as well as a brief discussion of some fields of work.

WINTER, H. M. AND WIECHELS, ARTHUR J. *How to Get a Good Job.* Cambridge: The Crimson Printing Company, 1960. $4.00. Written as a practical guide for those seeking all kinds of employment. Provides answers to a variety of specific questions based upon the experience and knowledge of the authors.

ZAREM, LEWIS. *Careers and Opportunities in Astronautics.* New York: E. P. Dutton. 1962. $3.95.

Directories, Bibliographies, and Handbooks

American Agencies Interested in International Affairs. New York: Council on International Affairs. $5.50. Lists approximately 300 organizations; gives the names of officers, purposes, founding dates, and other pertinent data. Revised periodically.

American Art Directory. Triennial. New York: R. R. Bowker Company. $22.50. In addition to museums, art schools, and art associations in the United States, it includes lists of art magazines, fellowships and scholarships, art schools abroad, and other art resources.

American Book Trade Directory. Triennial. New York: R. R. Bowker Company. $25.00. Lists all American and Canadian book publishers, subscription book publishers, dealers in foreign language books, book trade organizations, and many other resources in the field.

American College Public Relations Association Membership Directory. Annual. Washington, D.C.: American College Public Relations Association. $2.00. A membership directory of non-profit education institutions of higher learning and educational associations. Names and titles of the representatives are included.

American Junior Colleges. Edmund J. Glazer, Jr. (ed.) Sixth edition. Washington, D.C.: American Council on Education. $10.00. Descriptive data on 655 recognized junior colleges with information about staff, curricula, and other data. A useful resource for someone looking for a position in a junior college.

American Library Association Membership Directory. Annual. Chicago: American Library Association. $10.00. Directory of membership which includes such information as national, state, provincial, and local library associations, and agencies.

American Register of Exporters and Importers, Inc. Annual.

New York: American Register of Exporters and Importers. 5000 active American importers and exporters.

American Universities and Colleges. Ninth edition. Washington, D.C.: American Council on Education, 1965. $15.00. Descriptive material relative to accredited institutions.

American Voluntary and Non-Profit Agencies in Technical Assistance Abroad. New York: Technical Assistance Clearing House, American Council on Voluntary Agencies for Foreign Service. Contains 98 one-page profiles of American voluntary and non-profit agencies, including a list of executive officers, financial information, and outlines of their technical assistance activities. Revised periodically.

Art Direction Buyer's Guide of Art and Photography. Annual. New York: Art Direction. $1.00. Lists approximately 2,500 suppliers of art for advertising, illustrations, design, photography and graphic art services; includes classified listings, representatives, and studio listings, each giving address, telephone number and services performed. A possible source for contacts in the art field.

The Art School Directory. Biennial. New York: American Artists Magazine, Watson-Guptill Publications. $1.50. A fairly comprehensive listing of art programs in colleges and universities, specialized schools in the United States, Canada and abroad. Includes scholarship information.

Ayer's Directory of Newspapers and Periodicals. Annual. Philadelphia: N. W. Ayer & Son, Inc. $30.00. Lists over 20,000 newspapers and periodicals published in the United States and Canada. Gives important details for those interested in researching this field.

Book of the States. Biennial. Chicago: Council of State Governments. $9.00. Supplement, $3.00. Contains a list of state government officials and legislators and organizations; educational systems, health and welfare systems, judicial organizations, administrative systems, and similar information.

Boston's Directory of Research and Development Capabilities. Boston: Greater Boston Chamber of Commerce, 1963–64,

$5.00. A selective listing of companies in the Greater Boston area engaged in scientific research and development. Listings include degree distribution and areas of research and development.

BRADFORD, ERNEST S. *Bradford's Directory of Marketing Research Agencies in the United States and the World*. Eighth edition. New Rochelle, N.Y.: Bradford's Directory of Marketing Research Agencies, 1958–59.

Broadcasting Yearbook. Annual. Washington, D.C.: Broadcasting Publications, Inc. $5.00. Lists TV and Radio Stations in U.S., Canada, Mexico, and Caribbean. Includes advertisers and their agencies and names of executive personnel.

Career Planning Guide. Washington, D.C.: U.S. Dept. of Health, Education, and Welfare. Public Health Service.

Careers in World Affairs: At Home and Abroad. Compiled by Foreign Policy Association-World Affairs Center. New York: Doubleday, 1961. $1.75.

Catholic Press Directory. Annual. New York: Catholic Press Association. $3.00. Approximately 600 listings of Catholic newspapers and periodicals issued in the United States and Canada.

College Placement Annual. Annual. Bethlehem, Pennsylvania: College Placement Council, Inc. Lists employers and occupational openings for which they are recruiting, and occupational and geographical cross references. Includes a list of cooperating placement offices. Revised annually and distributed free of charge to college seniors or with a subscription to the *Journal of College Placement*.

College Placement Directory. O. T. ZIMMERMAN AND M. K. ZIMMERMAN (eds.). Fourth edition. Dover, New Hampshire: Industrial Research Services, Inc., 1965. $16.00. Lists American companies and government agencies which hire college graduates. Information is cross-indexed by job and geographic location. Companies offering foreign employment are identified by country and city.

Commonwealth of Massachusetts Industrial Directory. Compiled by the Bureau of Research and Statistics. Boston: Massachusetts Department of Commerce and Development, 1964. Listing of Massachusetts manufacturers according to the following classifications: alphabetical, geographic, and industrial.

Conservation Directory. Annual. Washington, D.C.: National Wildlife Federation. $1.00. Lists organizations and agencies concerned with the conservation, management, and use of this country's natural resources.

Dictionary of Occupational Titles. Prepared by the Division of Occupational Analysis, U. S. Employment Service. 2nd edition. Washington, D.C.: U.S. Government Printing Office.

Directory of American Council of Independent Laboratories. Washington, D.C.: American Council of Independent Laboratories. Free. Listing of laboratories. Entries include information on activities and senior scientific personnel. Revised biennially.

Directory of Catholic Facilities for Exceptional Children in the United States. Washington, D.C.: National Catholic Education Association. $2.75. Lists residential and day classes in operation for exceptional children in the Catholic School system in the United States. Periodic publication.

Directory for Exceptional Children. Fifth edition. Boston: Porter Sargent Publishers, 1965. $7.00. Lists educational and training facilities for children who require specialized programs. Includes national associations, federal and state government agencies and their personnel involved in special education.

Directory of Historical Agencies in the United States and Canada. Biennial. Madison: American Association for State and Local History. $1.75. Lists historical commissions, departments of archives and history, state and local historical associations, historical libraries, and other resources in this field.

Directory of Home Economists in Business. Annual. St. Louis: American Home Economics Association. $5.00. Lists agencies, associations, manufacturers, publications, radio and TV stations represented by the business group.

Directory of Overseas Schools in Europe, Asia, Africa, and the Middle East. Biennial. New York: International Schools Foundation. $2.00. Lists approximately 100 schools enrolling Americans (non-military). Entries include details about schools.

Directory of Scientific Resources in the Washington, D.C. Area. Washington, D.C.: $2.00. Lists research and development organizations, social and psychological science groups, documentation, operations research and computer specialists, and federal government laboratories. Revised periodically.

Directory of Social and Health Agencies of New York City. Community Council of Greater New York, Inc. New York: Columbia University Press. $10.00. Directory provides information about governmental and voluntary welfare and health agencies serving New York City.

Directory of Special Libraries. New York: Special Libraries Association. $5.00. Lists all special libraries in the U.S., Canada, and overseas. Published irregularly.

Directory of University Research Bureaus and Institutes. First edition. Detroit: Gale Research Company, 1960. $20.00. A guide to college and university sponsored bureaus, institutes, experiment stations, laboratories, and other research organizations established on a permanent basis and carrying on a continuing research program.

Encyclopedia of Associations. Frederick G. Ruffner, Jr. (ed.). Detroit: Gale Research Company, 1965. $22.50. First published in 1956 under the name of Encyclopedia of American Associations. Includes trade, business, professional, labor, scientific, educational, fraternal and social organizations of the U.S.

Fellowships in the Arts and Sciences. Robert Quick (ed.). Ninth edition. Washington, D.C.: American Council on Education, 1966–67. $2.25.

Florida Electronics Directory. Annual. Tallahassee: Florida

Development Commission. Free. Contains information on electronic, aircraft, missile, nuclear, and scientific instrument research in the state.

Foreign Language Press List. Annual. New York: American Council for Nationalities Service. $5.00. Entries include newspapers and magazines catering to ethnic groups, foreign language newspapers as well as data on the foreign language press.

The Foundation Directory. New York: Russell Sage Foundation. $10.00. Contains descriptive listings of over 5,000 foundations including general purpose and activities. Revised periodically.

From Campus to Career. New York: New York State Employment Service. $.60. A career guide planned to help the liberal arts graduate relate his academic background and interest to the world of work.

Gebbie Press House Magazine Directory. Triennial. New York: Gebbie Press, Inc. $19.95. Describes approximately 4,000 company magazines. Magazines are indexed into 63 different industries.

Governmental Research Association Directory. Biennial. New York: Governmental Research Association. $5.00. Lists over 1,000 individuals and organizations professionally engaged in doing research for federal governmental agencies.

Graduate Education: An Annotated Bibliography. James H. Blessing (ed.). OE-5000-22, Bulletin 1961, No. 26. Washington, D.C.: U.S. Government Printing Office, 1961. $.60. A comprehensive bibliography of sources covering the history and nature of graduate education, organization and administration, graduate programs, and other useful information.

Guide to American Directories. Bernard Klein (ed.). Sixth edition, New York: McGraw-Hill Company. $25.00. A guide to the major business directories of the United States covering a wide variety of categories.

Guide to American Educational Directories. Bernard Klein

(ed.). Second edition. New York: McGraw-Hill Company. $22.50. A guide to the major educational directories of the U.S. Includes more than 1,300 entries arranged alphabetically by title under subject categories. Annotations are helpful in determining the nature of each directory.

Guide to Foreign Information Sources. Semi-annual. Washington, D.C.: Chamber of Commerce of the United States of America. $.25. Contains sources of information on foreign nations, addresses of foreign embassies, organizations and services offering information, and an annotated bibliography.

Handbook of Office of Education. Washington, D.C.: U.S. Department of Health, Education, and Welfare. A brief description of the organizations and activities of the Office of Education and career opportunities.

Handbook of Women Workers. Biennial. Women's Bureau, Department of Labor, 1965. $.55.

Health Careers Bibliography for Guidance Counselors. Marian Rampel (ed.). Trenton: The New Jersey Health Careers Service, 1964. $2.00. Includes a fairly representative listing of materials on health careers. Items were screened according to NVGA standards for preparing and evaluating occupational literature.

Health Organizations of the United States and Canada. Ithaca: Graduate School of Business and Public Admin., Cornell University. $10.00. Lists national, regional and state organizations involved with health and related fields in the United States and Canada.

Hospitals. Guide issue of the *Journal of the American Hospital Association,* Parts 1 and 2. Chicago: American Hospital Association. $2.50. Lists hospitals in the U.S. and Canada, names of administrators, size, services, and other pertinent information.

Hotel and Travel Index. Hollywood, Calif.: Elwood M. Ingledue. $6.00. Lists over 7,000 hotels and resorts throughout the world, travel agents, and other travel information. Seasonal, four times a year.

Industrial Research Laboratories of the United States. William W. Buchanan (ed.). 1965. Twelfth edition. Washington, D.C.: Bowker Associates, Inc. $25.00. Each entry gives the name and address of the laboratory, description of the research activity, and composition of the research staff.

International Organizations in the Social Sciences. New York: UNESCO Publications Center. $1.50. Describes briefly the activities of 18 non-governmental organizations serving UNESCO.

List of Concerns Interested in Performing Research and Development. Annual. Washington, D.C.: Small Business Administration. Free. Lists approximately 3,000 small firms doing research and development work in a variety of categories. Entries include the type of research or development in which firms specialize.

Literary Market Place. A Directory of American Book Publishers. Annual. New York: R.R. Bowker Company. $7.45. A comprehensive source of information about book publishers in the United States and Canada, advertising agencies, artists and art services, public relations services, press associations, and other allied fields.

A Manual on Certification Requirements for School Personnel in the United States. Triennial. Washington, D.C.: National Commission on Teacher Certification. National Education Association. $4.00. Covers requirements in the U.S., Puerto Rico, overseas dependent schools, territorial schools, and exchange and study abroad. It includes teacher education institutions and approved programs.

Moody's Industrial Manual. Annual. New York: Moody's Investors Service. Usually in main library.

Museums Directory of the U.S. and Canada. Biennial. Washington, D.C.: Joint publication of the American Assoc. of Museums and the Smithsonian Institution. $7.50. Listings cover the entire museum field and include the names of the directors, nature of the collection, publications, and other useful information.

Music Magazine: Musical Courier Annual Directory of the

Concert World. Evanston: Summy-Birchard Company. $5.00. Contains approximately 10,000 listings covering the U.S. and abroad. Entries include artist managers, concert managers, music publishers, recording firms, institutions offering music courses, and many other music resources.

National Institute of Health Scientific Directory and Annual Bibliography. Washington, D.C.: Department of Health, Education, and Welfare. $.50. Contains a directory of the professional staff members and a bibliography of the scientific and technical publications from the Institute's program of laboratory and clinical research.

National & International Employment Handbook for Specialized Personnel. 1960–61. 6th edition. World Personnel Service, Juvenal L. Angel, Director, New York World Trade Academy Press, Inc.

NVGA Bibliography of Current Occupational Literature. Washington, D.C.: Career Information Review Service of the National Vocational Guidance Association, American Personnel and Guidance Association, 1966. $1.00. A compilation of listings appearing in the Vocational Guidance Quarterly 1963–65. A useful reference for identifying certain types of career materials.

Occupational Literature. An Annotated Bibliography. Gertrude Forrester (ed.). Revised edition. New York: H. W. Wilson Company. 1964. $8.50. This bibliography brings together in a central index approximately 4,000 selected references to current occupational literature. One section describes the school and college information. Other sections annotate charts, posters, and graphic aids; textbooks for courses in occupations; materials designed to assist youth in developing sound vocational plans; references on the techniques of job seeking and job advancement; and publications devoted to the counselors' use of occupational information. Additional sections give information about studying and working abroad, and scholarships available.

Occupational Outlook Handbook. Biennial. Washington, D.C.: U.S. Dept. of Labor, Bureau of Labor Statistics, 1966–67.

Order from: Superintendent of Documents. $5.50. Employment information on occupations.

Official Catholic Directory. Annual. New York: P. J. Kennedy and Sons. Vol. 1, $12.00. Vol. II, $13.00. Lists Catholic personnel and establishments. Volume I covers the U.S. and Rome. Volume II covers Canada, Newfoundland, Great Britain, Australia, Ireland, New Zealand, Cuba, Mexico, Bermuda, and the Philippines.

Organizations and Institutions of the University of the State of New York: The State Education Department Handbook. Albany: State Education Department. Lists all schools and units of education in New York State approved by the Board of Regents.

Organizations, Publications, and Directories in the Mass Media of Communications. Biennial. Iowa City: School of Journalism, University of Iowa. $1.50. Lists organizations and their publications, business and professional publications, directories, names and addresses of state press and state broadcasting associations, and other useful information.

A Placement Officer's Guide to Foreign Employment and Teaching Opportunities for U.S. College Students. Prepared by International Opportunity Committee. New York: Metropolitan New York College Placement Officers Association, 1964. $1.00. Outlines the opportunities available through private and public agencies for employment, brief traineeships, summer work, and teaching outside the United States.

Poor's Register of Directors and Executives. Annual. New York: Standard & Poor's Corporation. Lists corporation executives.

Professional Opportunities in Social Security. Washington, D.C.: U.S. Department of Health, Education, and Welfare. Describes HEW utilization of actuaries, accountants, economists, analysts, and statisticians.

Profiles, Careers in the U.S. Department of Agriculture. Washington, D.C.: U.S. Government Printing Office. 1964. Full page descriptions of the services of the department and occupational descriptions of entering and advanced positions.

Psychiatric Clinics and Other Resources in the United States. New York: National Association for Mental Health, Inc. $1.25. Lists psychiatric clinics, mental health associations, state institutions, state government departments, VA Administration, and other federal mental hospitals.

The Public Welfare Directory. Chicago: American Public Welfare Association.

Rehabilitation Centers Today. Washington, D.C.: Department of Health, Education, and Welfare. $1.00. Lists 77 rehabilitation centers in the U.S. and Canada and gives information on their programs.

Scientific Resources in the San Francisco Bay Area. San Francisco: Cosmos Institute. $5.00. Lists research facilities in the San Francisco Bay area.

Social Work Opportunities Abroad. New York: National Association of Social Workers. A directory of over 100 organizations offering social work opportunities in foreign countries. Identifies the type of social work engaged in by the organization. Revised periodically.

Social Work Yearbook. New York: National Association of Social Workers. $8.50. Lists social work agencies in the U.S., Canada, and abroad. Covers private, governmental, voluntary social agencies. Revised periodically.

Sources of Information and Unusual Services. Triennial. New York. Information Directory Company. $2.95. Contains a listing of sources of information and services on over 500 subjects, including business, commerce and labor, health and the arts.

Summer and Long-Term Employment and Service Opportunities. New York: Council on International Educational Exchange. Free.

Teaching: A National Directory of Preparation Programs for Women College Graduates. Lewiston: Catalyst in Education. $1.00. Contains a comprehensive listing of undergraduate and graduate programs available to women preparing for teaching careers. Includes separate lists of internship programs.

Teaching Opportunities, a Directory of Placement Information. Lee M. Frederick. OE-26000-64, Circular 737. Washington, D.C.: U.S. Government Printing Office. 1964. $.30. Lists wide variety of sources of information in regard to teaching positions in public, private, and various special schools at all levels in the United States and abroad.

Thomas Register of American Manufacturers. Annual. New York: Thomas Publishing Company. Usually kept in the College Library.

U.S. Army Handbook for Counselors and Students, Army Occupations and You: U.S. Department of the Army, 1964. Gives duties, qualifications, and training, as well as related civilian jobs through 55 guidance briefs. Also included are an occupational index and cross index for related civilian jobs. Outlines reserve opportunities, pay, subsistence, retirement, and re-enlistment bonus.

Vacations Abroad, Courses, Study, Tours, Work Camps. Vol. XVII. Paris, France: UNESCO, 1965.

Where to Find Vocational Training in New York City. Helen C. Birtwell (ed.). 19th edition. New York: Vocational Advisory Service, 1970. $8.50. A directory of public and private schools and colleges which give some form of trade, commercial, technical, semi-professional training in preparation for a definite type of employment or for an occupational objective.

Work, Study, Travel Abroad. New York: United States National Students Travel Association, 1965.

The Writer's Handbook. Annual. Boston: Writer, Inc. $6.95. A directory of over 2,000 magazines and book publishers including editorial requirements. A comprehensive resource for free lance writers.

Writer's Market. Annual. Cincinnati: F. & W. Publishing Corporation. $5.95. Lists over 3,000 possible markets for writers, photographers, and artists. Requirements and other pertinent information are included.

Writer's Yearbook. Annual. Cincinnati: F. & W. Publishing Corporation. $1.00 paperbound. Lists approximately 1,000 possible markets for writers, photographers, and artists and includes pertinent information. Similar to the *Writer's Market* but less comprehensive.

Yearbook of American Churches. Annual. New York: National Council of Churches of Christ. $5.95. Lists over 200 religious bodies of all faiths, church-affiliated accredited colleges and universities, religious periodicals, service agencies, and other such sources.

Guides to Graduate Study

ADAMS, WALTER AND GARRATY, JOHN. *A Guide to Study Abroad.* Manhasset, New York: Channel Press, Inc., 1962. $5.95.

Aid-to-Education Programs of Some Leading Business Concerns. Fifth edition. New York: Council for Financial Aid to Education, Inc. $4.50.

American Institute of Planners. Washington, D.C., 1963. A mimeographed item about professional training with a list of all universities giving degrees in city, regional, etc. planning.

The Art School Directory. Biennial. Published for American Artists Magazine. New York: Watson-Guptill Publications. $1.50. Lists approximately 1,000 colleges, universities, junior colleges, and private art schools in the U.S., Canada, and abroad, plus individual teachers of art classes. Includes information on courses and scholarships.

Assistantships and Fellowships in Mathematics. Providence, Rhode Island: American Mathematical Society, January, 1964. Detailed survey of colleges and universities offering advanced degrees in mathematics, material about their assistantships, and a selected list of non-departmental scholarships and stipends in mathematics.

Canada—Awards for Graduate Study and Research. Ottawa: Canadian Universities Foundation, 1963. Primary emphasis is on graduate assistance for Canadians in Canada, but includes awards open to U.S. Citizens, and by U.S. colleges to Canadian citizens.

Careers in Health Physics Through Atomic Energy Commission Special Fellowships. Oak Ridge Institute of Nuclear Studies, Washington, D.C.: Oak Ridge Operation Office, 1963. A description of careers in health physics, graduate programs, and a directory of fellows.

Commonwealth Universities Handbook, 1965. London: The Association of Universities of the British Commonwealth, 1965. $14.70.

Educational and Cultural Exchange Opportunities. U.S. Department of State, July, 1963. A brief but excellent guide to benefits under the Fulbright-Hays Act for study, teaching, lecturing, research, or consulting abroad, as well as grants to citizens of other countries for study or observation in the United States.

FEINGOLD, S. NORMAN. *Scholarships, Fellowships, and Loans.* Vol. IV. Boston: Bellman Publishing Co., 1965.

Fellowships Offered by Foreign Governments, Universities, and Private Donors, 1967–68. New York: Institute of International Education. Free.

Financial Assistance Available for Graduate Study in Medicine. 7th edition, Evanston, Illinois: Association of American Medical Colleges, 1963. $4.00.

Financing Graduate Education. U.S. Dept. of Health, Education, and Welfare, Office of Education, 1965. 15 cents.

Graduate Business Education, Programs of. Princeton: Educational Testing Service, 1964–66. Describes programs and lists nearly 100 graduate programs in detail of the 19 member schools of the Policy Committee for the Admission Test for Graduate Study in Business. Revised periodically.

Guide to Graduate Study, Future Employment, and Summer Opportunities, 1963–64. New Haven: Yale University, 1964. A publication by the Office of Counseling and Placement at Yale, but has general utility.

Handbook on International Study for U.S. Nationals. New York: Institute of International Education, 1965. $3.00.

Help for Your College Education—New York State Education Department, 1964–65. Albany: Publications Unit, State Education Department, May, 1964. A pamphlet describing 6 types of financial aid granted by New York State for undergraduate, graduate, and professional study.

Journalism Educator, The (Directory Issue, Winter). Provo, Utah: American Society of Journalism School Administrators. Condensed information about departments and schools of journalism, as well as work shops, etc., in graphic arts, radio-television, etc.

Journalism Scholarship Guide. New York: Newspaper Fund, Inc., 1964. Lists about 1,000 undergraduate and graduate awards by university. Includes a bibliography. Free.

KEYES, K. M. R. (ed.). *International Handbook of Universities.* 3d ed. Paris: The International Associations of Universities, 1959. $13.50. Also available from the American Council on Education.

Law Schools and Bar Admission Requirements in the United States: Review of Legal Education. Chicago: American Bar Association. Lists approved law schools, enrollment, tuition, faculty, etc.

Library Education, Fellowships, Scholarships, Grants-in-Aid, Loan Funds, and Other Financial Assistance. Chicago: American Library Association, 1963. Lists accredited library schools and their financial aids, plus national, state, and local sources of financial aid.

McDANIELS, CARL. "Financial Aid for Guidance and Personnel Graduate Study, 1964–65," *The Personnel and Guidance Journal* (Washington, D.C.). Sept.–June, monthly. $10.00 a year. Extract listing financial aids in this area by university.

MAXWELL, BERNARD G. (ed.). *Current Financial Aid for Graduate Students.* Peoria, Illinois: College Opportunities Unlimited, Inc., 1964. $7.50.

Medical Colleges, Admission Requirements, 1969–70. Evanston: Association of American Medical Colleges. Annual. $4.00. Outlines admission requirements and procedures for 100 medical colleges. More information is available from the Pre-Medical Advisory Staff of the Division of Science and Mathematics, Evanston, Illinois.

Medical Scholarships and Loan Fund Programs. Chicago: American Medical Association, February, 1961. A geographical index of some financial aids for medical students, interns, and residents.

Modern Foreign Language Fellowship Program. NDEA Title VI and Related NDEA Projects. Catalog No. 5. U.S. Department of Health, Education, and Welfare, 1966. Describes awards at the undergraduate, graduate, and postdoctoral levels for study in languages other than French, German, Italian, or Peninsular Spanish.

National Defense Graduate Fellowships Graduate Programs, 1966–67. U.S. Department of Health, Education, and Welfare. Free.

NESS, FREDERICK W. (ed.). *A Guide to Graduate Study, Programs Leading to the Ph.D. Degree.* 3rd edition. Washington, D.C.: American Council on Education, 1965. $7.50.

OAS Fellowship Program. OAS Fellowship and Professorship program. Annual. Washington, D.C.: Pan-American Union. Free.

Physics, Graduate Assistantships and Fellowships in Academic Institutions for 1964–65. New York: American Institute of Physics. A bulletin of general and specific financial aids indexed by university, listing number of assistantships, fellowships, stipend, etc.

Preparation in School and College Personnel Work—Program and Course Offerings. U.S. Dept. of Health, Education, and Welfare. Office of Education. 1963. A directory prepared by the U.S. Office of Education to provide information about opportunities for academic preparation in school and college personnel work.

Programs for Education in the Sciences. Washington, D.C.: National Science Foundation, 1963. A general pamphlet treating the Foundation's programs in science education.

"Psychology, Educational Facilities, and Financial Assistance for Graduate Students, 1964–65." *American Psychologist.* Washington, D.C.: The American Psychological Association, Inc., 1965. Reprint, $1.00. A reprint indicating course and other requirements for admission to graduate programs in psychology which are described together with financial aids in the second portion of the report.

Public Administration, Graduate Study in. Circular No. 631. Washington, D.C.: U.S. Department of Health, Education, and Welfare, 1961. $1.25. Describes 145 graduate programs in public administration in 83 universities, including 96 M.A. programs and 45 Ph.D. programs.

QUICK, ROBERT (ed.). *Fellowships in the Arts and Sciences, 1965–66.* Annual. Washington, D.C.: American Council on Education, 1966. $2.25. Prepared in cooperation with the Council of Graduate Schools in the United States. Information about the awards sponsored by foundations, government agencies, professional and learned societies, industries, and others which may be used in support of graduate study in the United States.

Scholarships, Fellowships, Work-Study Plans for Graduate Social Work Education for Individuals Interested in Jewish Community Center Work as a Career. Annual. New York: Personnel Services, National Jewish Welfare Board. Free.

A Selected List of Major Fellowship Opportunities and Aids to Advanced Education for U.S. Citizens. Washington, D.C.: The Fellowship Office, Office of Scientific Personnel National Academy of Sciences.

Social Work Fellowships and Scholarships in the U.S. and Canada. Annual. New York: Council on Social Work Education. $1.00.

Study Abroad 1970–72. International Handbook of Fellowships, Scholarships, and Educational Exchange. Vol. XVIII. Paris, France: UNESCO.

Teaching Abroad. New York: Institute of International Education. Updated periodically. Free.

Teaching: A National Directory of Preparatory Programs for Women College Graduates. Englewood Cliffs: Prentice-Hall, 1964. $1.00. Brief descriptions of programs in education offered in all states. Includes M.A.T. programs with paid internships. Also a reading list for those interested in teaching.

Theological Schools in the United States and Canada. Dayton, Ohio: American Association of Theological Schools, 1964. Gives the affiliations, enrollment, faculty numbers, course of study, cost, financial aids, admission requirements, and distinctive characteristics of all member schools and associate schools.

U.S. Grants 1971–72 for Graduate Study. New York: Institute of International Education. Free. Summarizes study opportunities by country, fields of study, language requirements, academic schedule, and information about dependents.

Government Publications

Sources

Counselor's Guide to Occupational and Other Manpower Information: An Annotated Bibliography of Selected Government Publications. Bulletin No. 1421. U.S. Department of Labor, November 1964. $.50. An excellent listing of career and manpower information available from various government agencies and departments.

Occupational Outlook Service. Bureau of Labor Statistics. U.S. Department of Labor. Request list of free Occupational Outlook publications and have your name placed on mailing list.

Peace Corps, Washington, D.C., 20525. Ask for list of recent publications.

Publications of the Women's Bureau. U.S. Department of

Labor, Women's Bureau. Free. A request to be placed on the mailing list will ensure notification of new publications.

Directories, Handbooks, Guides

Careers for College Graduates with New York State Government. Albany: Field Recruitment Unit, New York State Department of Civil Service, September, 1965. Manual includes a description of most of the entrance positions and the means by which college seniors and graduates can enter the service.

Career Guide for Demand Occupations. Bureau of Employment Security. U.S. Department of Labor, 1965. $.30.

Dictionary of Occupational Titles. 2 Vols. U.S. Department of Labor, Bureau of Labor Statistics, 1966. Vol. 1, Definition of Titles, $5 per copy. Vol. 2, Occupational Classifications, $4.25 per copy.

Education Directory. U.S. Department of Health, Education, and Welfare. Office of Education (Annual). Under $5.00.

Part 1 State Governments
Part 2 Public School Systems
Part 3 Higher Education
Part 4 Federal Government

Federal Career Directory—A Guide for College Students. U.S. Civil Service Commission, 1966. $.55. Information on federal employment, application procedures, and general system. Job briefs both by title and by college major.

United States Government Organization Manual. U.S. Government Printing Office. $1.75 (GS 4.109:965). A valuable reference for information about government agencies. This publication is revised periodically.

Recommended Career Pamphlets

Careers—Federal Careers. Pamphlets compiled by Civil Service Regions. Describe benefits of federal agencies, beginning jobs, and addresses of federal government bureaus and departments employing college graduates.

Careers in Employment Security. U.S. Department of Labor. Describes beginning positions in the Bureau of Employment Security.

Career Pamphlets. Veterans Administration, Department of Medicine and Surgery. (24 pamphlets). Free.

Careers in Science, Mathematics, and Engineering: A Selected Bibliography. U.S. Department of Health, Education, and Welfare, 1961. Designed to suggest sources from which counselors, teachers, secondary school students, and others concerned with vocational guidance can obtain free and inexpensive career information.

Careers in the U.S. Department of the Interior. Revised edition. U.S. Department of the Interior, 1962. Describes the activities of the Interior Department as well as training programs and regular programs of the Department.

Employment Opportunities in the Atomic Energy Field. Bureau of Labor Statistics, U.S. Department of Labor, 1962. Provides brief descriptions and employment outlook information about major scientific, engineering technician, and skilled occupations in the atomic energy field.

Federal Jobs Overseas. Pamphlet #29. U.S. Civil Service Commission, 1964. $.10. Describes how overseas jobs are filled by nine departments of the federal government. Included are Departments of Agriculture, Air Force, Army, Navy, Commerce, Interior, State, and the Agency for International Development, Panama Canal Company, Peace Corps, and the U.S. Information Agency.

Internal Revenue Service Careers: U.S. Treasury Department, 1964. Outlines beginning positions with this agency.

Job Horizons for College Women in the 1960's. U.S. Department of Labor. A pamphlet with career suggestions and a list of professional organizations in 37 fields.

Occupational Outlook Report Series. Bureau of Labor Statistics, U.S. Department of Labor. (From 1963–64 Occu-

pational Outlook Handbook). Set of 109 reprints, $9.55
or single reprints from 5 to 15 cents each.

The Way to a Job in Government. Pamphlet #47. U.S. Civil
Service Commission, 1963. Outlines steps in applying for
Federal jobs under Civil Service.

Periodicals

Business Week. New York: McGraw-Hill (Weekly). $8.00.

Careers for You in Property-Liability Insurance. Chicago. The
Personnel Management Committee of the American Mutual Insurance Alliance.

Changing Times. Washington, D.C. (Monthly). $6.00.

"College and Career Articles." *Mademoiselle.* New York: Alumnae Advisory Center, Inc. $.25. $1.00 for the next five
articles. Also $7.50 for looseleaf binder containing over 50
reprints.

Forbes. New York: Forbes, Inc. (Twice monthly). $7.50.

Fortune. Chicago: Time, Inc. (Monthly). $7.50.

Journal of College Placement. Bethlehem: The College Placement Council, Inc. (4 times a year).

Occupational Outlook Quarterly. Bureau of Labor Statistics,
U.S. Department of Labor. 35 cents per copy or $1.25 an-
nual subscription. $1.75 foreign annual subscription. Sup-
plement to *Handbook,* published September, December,
February, and May.

Occupational Outlook Report Series. Washington, D.C.: Department of Labor.

New York Times. (Daily and Sunday supplements).

Printers' Ink Magazine. New York: Printers' Ink Magazine.

Saturday Review. New York: Saturday Review, Inc. (Weekly).

Vocational Foundation, Inc., Information Bulletin. 353 Park
Ave., S., New York. (Weekly—from September to June).
$2.00 per year. Information concerning education and
training, scholarships and fellowships, occupational material and job opportunities, etc.

The Wall Street Journal. New York: Dow Jones & Company, Inc. $26.00 yearly.

Additional Sources of Career Information

American Dietetic Association, 620 North Michigan Avenue, Chicago, Illinois. Several pamphlets on careers in the field of dietetics are available at low cost.

American Geological Institute, 1444 N. Street, N.W., Washington, D.C. Send for career booklets dealing with the earth sciences. Free.

American Home Economics Association. 1600 Twentieth Street, N.W., Washington, D.C. 20009. Several pamphlets on careers in the field of home economics are available at low cost.

Publications and Documents of The American Institute of Architects, 1735 New York Avenue, N.W., Washington, D.C. 20006. Free.

Source List for Careers in the Biological Sciences. American Institute of Biological Sciences, 3900 Wisconsin Avenue, N.W., Washington, D.C. 20016. Free.

American Library Association. 50 East Huron Street, Chicago, Illinois. Pamphlets at low cost, concerning careers in the library.

American Occupational Therapy Association, 250 West 57th Street, New York, New York. Will provide literature regarding the field, educational requirements, approved schools.

B'nai B'rith Occupational Brief Series. Vocational Service, 1640 Rhode Island Avenue, N.W., Washington 6, D.C. 35 cents each.

Careers. Box 135, Largo, Florida.
Career Guidance Service—September through May.
$30 per subscription.
Career Briefs—25 cents each.
Career Summaries—15 cents each.

Careers Research Monographs. The Institute for Research. Chicago, Illinois. 95 cents per single copy or $4.75 for group of five.

National Association for Music Therapy, Inc., P.O. Box 610, Lawrence, Kansas 66044. Materials concerning careers in Music Therapy.

National Commission for Social Work Careers, Jointly sponsored by Council on Social Work Education and National Association of Social Workers, 345 46th Street, New York, New York 10017. Send for brochure listing career opportunities.

Materials About Nursing as a Career. Committee on Careers, National League for Nursing, 10 Columbus Circle, New York, New York 10019. Free.

Occupational Abstracts. Personnel Services, Inc., Jaffrey, New Hampshire 03452. Single copies 50 cents or 25 cents for students. Complete set $15.

Occupational Index. Personnel Services, Inc., Jaffrey, New Hampshire. Subscription of 4 issues plus cumulative index, $7.50. Single copies, $2.

Career Briefs. Pratt Institute, Brooklyn, New York. Office of Information Services. Bi-monthly. Free. Ask to be put on mailing list.

An Occupational Guide to Public Relations. Public Relations Society of America, Inc., New York, New York. 1963.

Career Guidance, Public Relations Society of America, Inc., 845 Third Avenue, New York, New York 10032. Pamphlets at low cost on Public Relations.

Science Research Associates, Chicago, Illinois. Send for information concerning various briefs and employment opportunities.

CHAPTER 7

Psychological Testing
and Counseling

Diagnosis—Yesterday and Today

SOMEWHERE AROUND 400 B.C. a Greek by the name of Hippocrates was sure he had found the answer to predicting human behavior. He said the way a person acted could be ascribed to the four humors or fluids of the body. These body fluids were black bile, yellow bile, blood, and phlegm. For example, a person with a predominance of black bile would tend to be disturbingly quiet, calm, sad, and brooding; whereas one with a predominance of yellow bile would tend to be excited, irascible, and aggressive.

A thousand years later the humoral theory was forgotten, but there was a new certain-sure technique for the manager of men: phrenology. This was the art of judging an individual's personality from facial appearance, shape of head, size of feet. Hence, if you wanted a generous worker, you hired a man with big feet, and you avoided a man with shifty eyes for he was treacherous. Bumps on the head at various spots determined ability. For example, a bump over the ear signified distinctiveness; a bump on the top of the head, firmness. There are not very many disciples of phrenology left today.

Back in 1940, a researcher with an almost Messianic approach to this same problem, Dr. Sheldon, of somatotyping fame at Harvard, was sure he had found the answer to understanding human behavior. His approach to the problem was an analysis of body types and the correlation of personal characteristics with body type. For example, fatty boys (endomorphs, as he called them) were amiable, ate too much, and conformed to social conventions. Muscle men, on the other hand (or mesomorphs), were adventurous, dressed informally, withstood pain easily and willingly. Or, take the thin man, the bag of bones—the linear type—he was asocial, unamiable, liked only a few friends, disliked nude swimming, could not take pain, and was non-adventurous.

For years man has been searching for more reliable and valid measures of human behavior. The psychological test, it was hoped, would give us a more objective means of diagnosing behavior. Psychological tests, in their present form, are praised by some and damned by others.

What Psychological Tests Attempt to Do

Psychological tests may be helpful tools in guidance and counseling, if one keeps in mind their limitations. What the tests do is take samples of an individual's behavior (depending on what one wishes to learn)—a series of candid camera shots, if you will, which, when put together, give a composite picture of the individual. Typical behavior sampled might be the ability to work with mathematical detail, reading speed and comprehension, driver reaction time, understanding mechanical relationships, attitudes toward foreigners, vocational interests, space relations ability, and personality integration.

The psychologist does several things with his results: (1) diagnoses; (2) predicts; (3) controls. A very common example of these three objectives at work can be found in almost any classroom today. For example, so-called intelligence and scholastic aptitude tests might be used to diagnose an individual's educational strengths and weaknesses. Let us assume the tests (a) diagnose superior behavior in areas of scholastic performance. The psychologist might then (b) predict superior performance in the classroom. (c) To control or help insure superior performance, the individual might then be placed in a group of his peers.

Generally, when one talks about measurement, he thinks in terms of constant units of measurement. A foot, for example, is always 12 inches. Psychological measurement is not this exact. Not all the tests in psychology are quantitive. Some very useful guidance tests give only verbal descriptions of subjects—not numerical scores. Cronbach gives an acceptable definition: A test is a "systematic procedure for comparing the behavior of two or more individuals." [1] On the other hand, Noll says, "Not all methods of appraisal or evaluation in education are quantitative, but those which are not cannot properly be classified as measurement." [2] Thorndike once said, "If a thing exists, it exists in some amount, and if it exists in some amount it can be measured." [3] When test results are used, therefore, they should be considered as straws in the wind—objective checks of subjective opinion. Tests are not infallible, and the more complex the behavior measured, the more difficult to get precise measures of response.

Qualities of a Good Test

In the light of the foregoing, the reader may question, "Just how dependable are psychological tests anyway?" In an effort to refine measuring instruments, the psychologist subjects his findings to statistical analyses in order to determine how reliable and how valid his tests are. A test is reliable when it is consistent with itself. For example, if an individual receives an I. Q. score of 100 on a test today, can one be sure a similar alternate form of the test tomorrow will produce approximately the same 100 score? If the test is reliable, it will not produce a 100 I. Q. today and a 130 I. Q. tomorrow. It will be consistent.

If a test measures what it is supposed to measure, it is said to be valid. For example, high scores on scholastic aptitude tests such as the College Boards should equate with strong scholastic achievement. It is the responsibility of any test maker to conduct sufficient research in the selection of his test items and in the standardization of his test to assure a reasonable degree of validity. Here again it must be kept in mind that it is relatively easy to establish the validity of, say, a mathematics aptitude test, but extremely difficult to validate a test of personality or attitude.

Fields of Testing

Psychological tests are classified in a variety of ways. The following classification is functional so that the reader may know the purposes for which tests are designed:

1. Achievement Tests—Such tests seek to measure the individual's acquired knowledge in specific subject matter areas such as arithmetic, language usage, history, or what have you. Since the individual either knows or does not know the answers (i.e., there are either right or wrong answers), achievement tests are the most reliable and valid tests available.

Typical achievement test batteries (groups of tests) are the Stanford Achievement Tests, the Metropolitan Achievement Tests, the Iowa Every-Pupil Tests of Basic Skills, Iowa Tests of Educational Development, California Achievement Tests, Cooperative General Achievement Tests.

Achievement test results are particularly valuable in two areas of individual counseling: (1) They make possible standards of comparison so that one knows how an individual compares with others; and (2) By giving this comparison, one can learn where the individual's achievement strengths and weaknesses lie. Test results then become of value in establishing remedial action.

2. Aptitude Tests—Since one can never get inside a person, his ultimate capacity or his maximum potential in any area can never really be known. One can only measure aptitude—those characteristics which develop in an individual—independent of training. Warren, in his *Dictionary of Psychology,* defines aptitude as a "condition or set of characteristics indicative of ability to learn." [4] Aptitude tests are given, therefore, to try to measure untrained potential with a view to predicting what might happen if training followed. There are tests of general scholastic aptitude (among which are the so-called intelligence tests) and tests for more specific abilities such as mechanical aptitude, space relations aptitude, clerical aptitude, musical aptitude, art aptitude. Some of the better known general scholastic aptitude tests are the Stanford Binet Test of Intelligence, the Wechsler-Bellevue Scales of Mental Ability, the American Council on Education Psychological Examinations, the Army General Classification Test, the Otis Self Administering Tests of Mental Ability, the California Short Form Test of Mental Maturity, the CEEB Test of Scholastic Aptitude, the Graduate Record Examination; these are all measures of so-called intelligence or scholastic aptitude. Well-known tests in areas of special abilities are the Minnesota Paper Form Board (space relations), the Bennett Test of Mechanical Comprehension (mechanical relationships), Minnesota Clerical Aptitude (speed and accuracy in handling clerical detail), the Seashore Measure of Musical Talents (pitch, rhythm, tonal memory, etc.), Meier Art Judgment Test (aesthetic judgment), the Purdue Pegboard, and the O'Connor Finger and Tweezer Dexterity Tests (manual dexterity), to mention a few.

Coefficients of correlation of reliability and validity must be carefully checked before using aptitude tests. A reliable and valid test instrument can serve as a piece in the jigsaw puzzle picture of an individual. One of the problems of aptitude testing is that the individual who has had training in things mechanical or in drawing, for example, will test higher in mechanical aptitude and space relationships. Which, then, is the test measuring, achievement or aptitude?

Despite their limitations, aptitude tests can be of value; their value is limited to the intelligent interpretation of the test results.

3. Interest Measures—Interest inventories serve a relatively simple purpose: to measure a person's likes and dislikes in a variety of situations. What interest tests do is to compare the interests of the individual being tested with various vocational group interest patterns already established through research. The primary use of the interest inventory is to aid in the selection of courses of study and in vocational choice. Among the well-known measures of vocational interest are the Kuder Preference Record, the Strong Vocational Interest Blank, the Cleeton Vocational Interest Inventory.

The Strong VIB is a carefully developed, experimentally derived test. The 400 items in the inventory produce 50 occupational interest areas for men. The Kuder inventory presents 168 sets of forced choices; Kuder is used widely with high school students; the Strong VIB is strictly an adult test.

Several problems make the use of interest inventories hazardous. In the first place, research reveals that individuals tend to react negatively to things they do not know about or do not understand. Further, interest inventories can be manipulated by an intelligent person to produce the results he wishes to produce. Hence, scores can be easily distorted. Another common problem arises from misinterpretation of results. The inventory may produce high scores, say, in areas of mathematics and science, whereas the subject may have little mathematics and science achievement or aptitude. Yet, invariably, the high mathematics and science interest scores tend to push a person in the direction of investigating related academic and vocational areas, despite his possible lack of aptitude. Perhaps the greatest problem of all in interest measurement of the college student is revealed by Strong researchers. They warn that interests remain extremely dynamic through the college years. The use of interest inventories at the college level is, therefore, of dubious value. It can be seen, then, that pre-college interest measurement is of questionable value.

Placement educators who wish to use interest inventories need be especially alert to their fallibility; interpretations must be made in the light of other pertinent personal, educational, and vocational information.

4. Personality and Attitude Tests—The area of personality measurement is one of the most chaotic in all the fields of measurement; it is an area in which tests are least well refined, yet where claims for interpretation are most boastful. Many tests currently in use are neither reliable nor valid. Hence the need for considerable discretion in this area of measurement.

What the measures of personality attempt is to diagnose and describe the individual in terms of his personal traits, how well he relates both to himself and to society.

Among more widely used tests are the Bernreuter Personality Inventory, the Rorschach Inkblot Test, the Minnesota Multiphasic Personality Inventory, and the Murray Thematic Apperception Test.

Related to the measurement of personality traits are attitude testing and opinion surveys. These attempt to measure feelings ranging all the way from attitudes toward communism, Negroes, labor unions, peace and war, to those toward birth control, the Democratic and Republican Parties, and whether a person is in the frame of mind to make major purchases of goods like autos and refrigerators. Here again, counselors are on shaky ground as some of the pollsters will readily confess.

Personality tests cannot be quantified statistically. Few personality tests produce numerical scores. Under no circumstances should the placement educator attempt personality test interpretation without adequate study in the psychology of personality, abnormal psychology, and tests and measurements. Personality test interpretation depends almost wholly upon the psychological orientation of the examiner. The placement counselor who wants information about the personality of his counselee will probably find a carefully structured interview of greater value to him than the personality test.

The Problem of Testing: "Quantaphrenetics"

There is value in many tests; sometimes group behavior can be predicted in areas of aptitude and achievement testing; and sometimes the behavior of individuals can be predicted with some degree of accuracy through the use of scores at the extremes. But, at best, tests are only straws in the wind. The trouble comes when education, government, and business use tests as if they are really infallible, scientific instruments. And tests are being used this way by both education and industry. A recent nationwide survey of 852 companies made by the Bureau of Business Research of the University of Texas indicated that 56 per cent of the companies sampled are using personality tests for the purpose of hiring and upgrading. The magazine *American Business* in a parallel survey found a similar percentage of use. *Fortune* made a survey of 63 firms. Sixty per cent said they are using tests for hiring and upgrading.

Martin Gross in *The Brain Watchers* [5] says that more than 10,000,000 employees have already had their psyches probed and that more than a million a year are now being tested. Science Research Associates, a test bureau in Chicago, now has 11,000 industrial clients and many more school system clients.

One gets into trouble by attempting to predict success in school, on the job, and in life on the basis of aptitude and achievement tests. In his book *Excellence* [6] John W. Gardner explains that any system of identification of talent which assumes achievement and aptitude tests to be perfect will commit grave mistakes, the worst, perhaps, by trying to apply the results beyond the performances for which the tests were designed. The temptation is to lean heavily on tests which do not pretend to measure such qualities as attitudes, values, motives, and non-academic talents. Difficulties arise when trying to predict expected performance in life. Persons with a high degree of some of the as-yet-unmeasurable traits such as zeal, judgment, and staying power, may achieve more success later in life than a person with high test scores but lacking these traits.

Gardner cites the case of Rennie, a most gifted child, very articulate, quick in school, but also lazy, self-indulgent, flaccid, and infantile in his emotions and personality. This did not reflect in his school work. He ultimately graduated from college with honors, but in the 20 years thereafter, he did not do a thing. While this boy had a high degree of scholastic aptitude, he must have been quite lacking in the ingredients necessary for success in adult life.

That great British theologian, Monsignor Knox, describes an individual in this way:

> "To the statistician, the mass observer, you are a unit in a crowd. To the physicist, you are a mathematical formula; to the chemist, a compound of substances; to the biologist, a specimen. The behaviorist sees you as an animal modified by conditioned reflexes; the psychologist, as a mental type suffering, to a more or less degree, from morbid variations; the philosopher, as the subject of conscious experience. You interest the historian as one of the innumerable insects that build up the coral island of human development; the economist, as a bee or drone that helps cross-fertilize the cycle of production and consumption. To the postman, you are an address; to the politician, a voter; to the Bureau of Internal Revenue, a taxpayer." [7]

It is important to keep in mind that an individual is appreciably more than the sum total of his psychological test results. There is a place for psychological testing in career counseling. The test is one of the pieces of information gathered about the counselee to help him better understand himself. Neither the counseled nor the counselor can abrogate responsibility for decision to the tests. There is no substitute for the personal interview and the cataloging and interpretation of past achievement, life experiences, and test results in the light of the interview. Personnel data cannot be fed into a computer and left to the tests and the machines for a decision. Personnel administration, educational or otherwise, is not a science; it is an art.

(*Turn page for bibliography*)

BIBLIOGRAPHY

[1] Cronbach, Lee J., *Essentials of Psychological Testing*, Harper & Brothers, N. Y., 1949, p. 11.

[2] Noll, Victor H., *Introduction to Educational Measurement*, Houghton Mifflin Co., Boston, 1957, p. 9.

[3] Cronbach, op. cit., p. 12.

[4] Warren, H. C., *Dictionary of Psychology*, Houghton Mifflin Co., Boston, 1934.

[5] Gross, Martin L., *The Brain Watchers*, Random House, New York, 1962, p. 7.

[6] Gardner, John W., *Excellence*, Harper & Brothers, 1961, pp. 49–50.

[7] Farwell & Peters, *Guidance Readings for Counselors*, from a paper on "Testing: Boon or Scandal" by Morley Mays, p. 227, Rand McNally & Co., Chicago, 1961.

CHAPTER 8

Automation in Placement

The Numbers Problem in Placement and Recruitment

MOST PLACEMENT OFFICERS will say that they are understaffed and overworked by administrative minutiae caused by constantly increasing enrollments on the one hand, while, on the other hand, a burgeoning economy has created an insatiable appetite for college graduates on the part of employers. The placement office is caught in the middle. Bogged down in a morass of paper detail just to get the day's work done, the real job of placement, namely counseling, often never gets done satisfactorily, if at all. Something is going to have to give!

Recruitment by industry, as currently pursued, is extremely expensive. A. F. Hartford, manager of College Relations for DuPont, has said that "College recruiting is the most inefficient and costly phase of a company's staffing operation. . . . We'd go out of business if the rest of our company had to be run the same way." [1]

For a long time some placement educators and company recruiters have maintained there must be a better way both for the placement office to process student job hunters and for companies to recruit. Raymond H. Stockard, a past president of the

College Placement Council and placement director at the University of Rhode Island, has said, ". . . a face-to-face confrontation (student and prospective employer) is a waste of time for both the recruiter and the student if the recruiter is merely using the initial interview as a screening session and is using a definable set of criteria which could be applied mechanically prior to the interview . . . the sheer weight of numbers will eventually make it impossible for recruiters to talk to every candidate on every campus who wants to see them. There seems to be no alternative but to find some means for bypassing the time, effort, and space-consuming, if not inefficient, elementary screening of the campus interview." [1]

Some believe the computer has the potential to rescue both the placement officer and the recruiter. Why has this application been developing so slowly? Among several reasons are the increasing fears of further impersonalization at the multiversity; there is also the losing battle on the small college campus to keep relationships intimate. Even so, it is predicted that one common denominator, namely the cost of doing business, will force both placement educator and recruiter into a computerized operation.

Advocates believe that the computer properly utilized, as a tool and not as master, can aid both college and company. The placement educator can be relieved of arduous detail and, at the same time, be set free to do the most important job of all in placement; namely, counseling which, in turn, can help personalize, not depersonalize, the placement services.

How Can the Computer Improve and Help Personalize Placement Operations?

The computer can handle far better than the clerical worker the job of storing and retrieving data; furthermore, the computer is always accurate; it does not forget; it is capable of total recall in dealing with endless numbers of students and infinite combinations of data about these students. Most placement officers, even in today's small college, cannot select from memory accurately all those students and alumni registered who might meet the needs of a particular employer. The computer can do this.

The computer can store data on each student such as his interests, abilities, personality pattern, his achievement record, part-time job experiences, geographical preference, personal, extracurricular, and academic data, job areas in which he is interested, etc. It can also store company data about jobs available, the qualities sought in candidates—majors, degrees, geographical preference, and the like. When job notices are received, or recruiter schedules are to be prepared, the computer can be instructed to select those applicants whose stored data patterns match the job requirements of the employer. It will take but seconds for the computer to complete such a search and print out a list of candidates available.

Once the data bank stores information, the computer can be programmed to retrieve these data in an endless variety of combinations. Already a great many programs are available from time-sharing service bureaus which can be readily adapted to placement needs. The fact is that in the large placement operation, manual procedures for screening and selecting candidates to recommend to prospective employers are inadequate, costly, and cannot help but be incomplete.

Another equally time-saving application of the computer could be the dispensing of company-job information. For example, a student might wish to know what kinds of jobs are available for accountants, or anthropologists, or home economics majors, and what companies hire for these jobs and where. The student could identify himself and any restrictions (geographical, type of company, etc.) to the computer very simply, and within seconds he could have a print-out of the information desired. He is, then, ready to go to the placement office library and commence his learning about employers that might be interested in him. Such a procedure would save countless hours of counselor and clerical time, time which the counselor could use to get down to counseling.

How Does Data Get Into the Computer?

First of all the placement office must decide what data it wishes to collect and in what detail it wishes to identify its candidates. The data collecting procedure had best be designed to be easily coded for electronic data processing. The medium may be punched Hollerith cards, punched paper tape, or magnetic tape. These data may now be entered directly into the computer and stored in the proper computer file.

A similar information file to describe company positions available must be organized and stored in its proper computer file.

To activate the job-screening process, all the placement officer has to do is to read into the computer a position description. The computer then scans the student qualifications file and matches qualified students to position descriptions. In but a few seconds, the computer will cause the placement office terminal to print out a list of registrants already stored in the machine who match position requirements. The process is the same whether you are searching for a company or a student.

Using the Computer as a Student Motivator

Upon completion of its selection procedures, the computer can be programmed to do yet another job for the placement office, whether it has local access directly to the computer or is "on-line" with a terminal. The computer can address and type letters to those students whom it has selected for interviews, thus notifying them personally of their selection, the time and place of the interview, and the name of the interviewer, and inviting them to sign up.

The University of Arkansas has used the computer to help counter student apathy in signing up for job interviews. On the

subject of student apathy in job interviewing, the late Neil
Harmon had this to say:

> "In the past, our methods of informing students
> about recruiters' visits included: (a) weekly notices
> in the student newspaper; (b) colored placards
> posted on bulletin boards throughout campus;
> (c) weekly notices sent to heads of departments;
> and (d) a schedule released early each semester
> listing the names of companies and agencies and
> the disciplines they would be seeking.
>
> "There had been a noticeable lack of interest in
> job-seeking among graduates from the College of
> Arts and Sciences, our largest group of graduates.
> Investigation revealed the need for better com-
> munication . . . we decided that a personal ap-
> proach rather than mass communication, should
> be used . . ."[2]

Arkansas settled for individualized letter writing by the computer. How did the students react? Thirty per cent more students signed up for interviews; greater use of employer literature was observed; there were fewer sign-ups on wrong schedules. A questionnaire to the students on whether they wished
the system to be continued brought an 80 per cent response.[2]

An Automated Career Planning Library

Aysel Searles, placement director at the State University of
New York at Binghamton, observes that with more than 2,400
occupations requiring at least the baccalaureate degree, the
student is sometimes hard pressed to locate appropriate literature.[3] The Binghamton office has, therefore, undertaken the
project of coding occupational information by interest areas
on punched cards.

Punched card data could then be transferred to the computer

to increase the speed of a search. Presumably, were the place-ment office to computerize its occupational information services, the student would simply call for material in certain occupa-tional areas; he would then get an instant print-out of the list of materials for which he searches. His next step, of course, would be to sign out from the occupational library those materials in which he is interested.

What If You Have No Computer?

Few placement offices can justify rental costs on a computer installation. However, time-sharing rentals are well within the budgets of many placement offices. In time-sharing, one may either rent or purchase a terminal which in effect is a tele-type-writer. Being "on-line" (with the computer) allows the place-ment office to use the terminal which both transmits and re-ceives information via telephone to and from the computer. The computer need not be nearby; it can be hundreds of miles distant. Time-sharing has suddenly become big business because it gives the little fellow a chance at the computer.

Clusters of colleges could easily form cooperative pools to share computer information and thereby cut costs. For example, occupational information of the sort being collected by the State University of New York at Binghamton could be readily shared. Colleges could easily share the same company-positions-available file within a computer, thus leaving the college only the student file to develop, and thereby save the cost of dupli-cating company files.

Placement educators interested in freeing themselves of cler-ical detail and thereby gaining time for counseling activities are urged to investigate computer time-sharing.

If the reader believes there is an insufficient volume of work on his campus to justify the use of the computer on any basis, Bond [4] suggests that "the same end result can be achieved by an alternate system . . ." In this system no computer is used; rather, the job is done by sorting punched cards. The card-sort system requires that registration data be collected, coded, and key punched into IBM cards. These cards are then fed into a sorting machine which in a series of progressive sorts keeps eliminating cards until the final sort reduces the number of registrant cards to those which match the job requirements.

Since it is possible to print whatever data one wishes on the IBM card, the card is readily identifiable. Obviously, one is restricted here to the speed of the sorter. However, this is an inexpensive way for the small placement office to do a better job of handling its clerical detail. One needs but two pieces of relatively inexpensive equipment to initiate this system: a key punch and a card sorter.

Computer Costs

A key punch and a low-speed sorter can each be rented for less than $100 per month. These could meet the needs of a small placement service.

However, there is a considerable step in cost effectiveness when the placement office ties into a time-sharing system, and especially when several colleges group together to share the employer information file in a time-sharing program. This is the underlying goal of time-sharing—to reduce the cost of computer rental by sharing its facilities among the users.

The approach of vendors to costing for time-sharing varies greatly, and no one set of figures can be provided as a completely accurate indication of expense. A placement office contemplating an "on-line" time-sharing installation would have to consider the following items (the costs are estimates based on 1969–70 figures): (a) a terminal (teletypewriter) which rents for about $120 per month; (b) computer time which ranges from $15–$75 per hour, depending on type of service (it is estimated that costs would run at approximately $1 per company or student search); (c) computer file storage costs which average about $2 per 1,000 characters per month. To illustrate, let us assume one wishes to build and store in the computer a file on 250 companies and a file on 100 students. Allowing 6 items to identify one position for each of 250 companies (such as name of company, location, position, salary, major, degree requirement) and 15 items to identify each of 100 students (such as name of student, age, sex, major, degree, extracurricular activities, part-time jobs, and so on), storage costs to maintain the 250-company file would be about $5 per month. It would also cost another $5 per month to store the 100-student file.

There is a fourth item of cost, namely that of a telephone line. Separate telephone lines for terminals are not necessary. However, if present lines available are used, it must be remembered that when the placement office is "on-line" to the computer, that particular line is tied up. It should also be remembered that, without a Watts line, standard long-distance telephone rates pertain.

More specific cost answers cannot be given here. Any timesharing service bureau will be glad to give the placement office both counsel on how to develop a placement program on an economical basis as well as cost estimates.

Evaluation of Computer Use in Placement

There is considerable evidence accumulating at a growing number of institutions that electronic data processing can relieve the placement office of mounds of paper work in the placement-recruitment process. "At UCLA the man-hours required to collect and process data have been reduced by almost 40 per cent" by the computer, allowing . . . "more time for interviewing and counseling of students and alumni . . ." [5]

The fears extant that computerization of the placement office might depersonalize placement-student-employer relationships have not materialized. Quite a contrary condition has been produced where electronic data processing has been tried. The computer has, rather, greatly increased the effectiveness of professional staff members.

BIBLIOGRAPHY

1 Kauffman, Warren E., "Senior Placement—The Story of a Successful Three-Year Experiment by a Large Firm and a University," *Journal of College Placement*, April–May, 1967, pp. 43 ff.

2 Harmon, Neil, "Arkansas Uses Computer to Help Curb Apathy Toward Interviews," *Journal of College Placement*, February–March, 1967, p. 57.

3 Searles, Aysel, "A Computerized Career-Planning File Leads Students to 'Self Help,'" *Journal of College Placement*, December–January, 1968, pp. 38–39.

4 Bond, Charles L., "The Computer: Time Saver for Busy Directors," *Journal of College Placement*, April, 1963, p. 62.

5 Scully, Joseph R., "UCLA EDP—a Placement Office Implements a Complete Computer System," *Journal of College Placement*, December, 1967–January 1968, p. 70.

SUGGESTED READINGS

RICHARDSON, ALLAN D., "Automation in the Placement Office"—a study made by the EDP Research Committee of the Southwest Placement Association, January, 1967, 49 pp., $1.00. Write: President, Southwest Placement Association.

"Computers in Higher Education"—report of the President's Science Advisory Committee, The White House, Washington, D. C. February, 1967, 79 pp. Available from Superintendent of Documents, U. S. Government Printing Office, 30 cents.

Special Report: "Computers on College Campuses," *College Management*, April, 1967, pp. 39–46.

CHAPTER 9

The Problems of
Effective Communication

THE COUNSELOR MUST UNDERSTAND the student and his
needs if there is to be meaningful communication. The
Berkeley, the Columbia, and the Wisconsin situations, and a
great many less well publicized confrontations like them, are
symptomatic of the communications problems that confront
college administrators. A particular issue which disturbs many
reflective youth is the lack of relevancy to life of what goes on
within the university. In a nationally televised program, a panel
of distinguished college presidents discussed this question of
relevancy with an especially knowledgeable group of students.
The classics came under student fire. An erudite president
defended with eloquence the relevancy of the classics to modern
life. A student spokesman, interrupting, said, "You see, Mr.
President, we wholeheartedly agree with you, but your own
faculty has us doing no more than parsing sentences, memo-
rizing, and regurgitating."

College students are not only at war with sterility of education; they are at war with the system, itself. The outrage of the
Kennedy assassinations, the collapse of Johnson's Great Society,

the interminable war in Vietnam, the university's involvement in war-related research, and the consequent drain of national resources away from solving the problems of the ghetto and the polluted environment have eroded the trust of college youth in The Establishment. Education is very much a part of the The Establishment, and it is not doing a very good job of communicating with its youth.

Understanding—A Prerequisite to Communication

Communication is the meaningful exchange of ideas. Much of our communication is designed to produce behavior responses. Too often communication fails because the perceptions of the counselor differ quite markedly from the perceptions of the student. For example, the counselor perceives the company recruiter as a bearer of good tidings, a source of fine job opportunities. And the counselor perceives these jobs as opportunities to be examined and considered ever so carefully. Here is where it becomes difficult for those over 30 to realize that the symbolic realities of those under 30 are not the realities of those over thirty. For many young people the symbols of opportunity—a good job with a chance to make a top starting salary—are symbols of yesterday, meaningless in an age of affluence. For this group the symbols today are napalm, rat-infested ghettos, the ashes of Christianity.[1] Because student physical needs are so well met by parent, college, and government, students see as their needs to fulfillment a society without wars and ghettos, a society which really does guarantee freedom and give equal opportunity to every individual, a society which will do something about its ecological problems. To these ends they react to communication, and not to much else.

From psychology we learn that what the organism sees or hears is conditioned by the perceiver's self-image; and that self-image is determined by how the organism's needs are met. These needs may be to escape from the draft or to relate meaningfully to a society torn apart by racial strife. Serious conflict may develop within the individual's value system as he looks, on the one hand, at a comfortable job in The Establishment and, on the other hand, at the challenge of the underdeveloped areas of the world and the ghettos here at home.

Unless the counselor, therefore, really understands the student's values, hopes, and aspirations, how can the counselor possibly communicate?

Joseph Kauffman, when dean of student affairs at the University of Wisconsin, observed that:

> "The new college student . . . looks at the big university, the big government, big business, big labor, big research enterprise, and the big church with considerable dismay, and asks with a mixture of Martin Buber and Sören Kierkegaard, 'Where in all this bigness and impersonality is there room for my lonely suffering soul; where can I find a meaningful I–Thou dialogue?'
>
> "The new student wants solidarity, participation, and fellowship, unequivocally and passionately. But he views most organizations of our computerized, bureaucratized, rationalized, formalized, urban, industrial society as, almost by their nature, inimical to the freedom and spontaneity of the human spirit . . . in practice many of the organizations with which they come in contact seem subtly depersonalizing; few provide any real community." [2]

We must first understand these students before communication is possible.

How Perceptions Influence Language Meaning

The individual is the sum of all his yesterdays. The meanings which he gives to his perceptions depend, then, on how the environment has conditioned him. Contrast, if you will, the

differences in meaning which blacks and whites give to the
same situation in the "Ballad of the Landlord" by the late
Afro-American poet, Langston Hughes: [3]

Landlord, landlord
My roof has sprung a leak.
Don't you 'member I told you about it
Way last week?

Landlord, landlord
These steps is broken down.
When you come up yourself
It's a wonder you don't fall down

Ten bucks you say I owe you?
Ten bucks you say is due?
Well, that's ten bucks more'n I'll pay you
Till you fix up this house new.

What? You gonna get eviction orders?
You gonna cut off my heat?
You gonna take my furniture and
Throw it in the street?

Um-huh! You talking high and mighty
Talk on—till you get through.
You ain't gonna be able to say a word
If I land my fist on you.

Police! Police!
Come and get this man!
He's trying to ruin the government
And overturn the land.

Coppers whistle!
Patrol bell.
Arrest.

Precinct station.
Iron cell.
Headlines in press:

Man Threatens Landlord
Tenant held; No Bail
Judge gives Negro 30 days in
County Jail.

These lines readily suggest how experience determines what we perceive.

Charles S. Isaacs, a bright young white teacher at New York City's J.H.S. 271, has suggested that if we wish to understand the 1968 New York teachers' strike, all we have to do is to "replace the landlord with the educational establishment, the tenant with the black parent, and the leaky roof with a history of inferior education—then write a sequel to Langston's poem." [4]

In the words of one communications specialist, James Schwartz, "the meanings we have for events are our expectations about them—what they will and will not do, how they relate to other events, what difference they make to our daily lives." [5] In this context, for example, does the white really understand what the black is saying today?

Schwartz calls attention to this long-standing classical problem of the meaning of words by recalling the conversation between Humpty-Dumpty and Alice in Lewis Carroll's "Through the Looking Glass": [5]

"I don't know what you mean by 'glory,' " Alice said.

Humpty-Dumpty smiled contemptuously, "Of course you don't—'til I tell you. I meant 'there's a nice knockdown argument for you!' "

"But glory doesn't mean 'a nice knockdown argument,' " Alice objected.

"When I use the word," Humpty-Dumpty said in a rather scornful tone, "it means just what I choose it to mean—nothing more or less."

"The question is," said Alice, "whether you can make words mean so many different things."

"The question is," said Humpty-Dumpty, "which is to be master—that's all."

If Humpty-Dumpty seems a bit other-worldish, then think about the word "democracy" and how it is used in and what it means to the Communist countries.

We can never be quite sure what we perceive. Alice and Humpty-Dumpty saw quite different things in the word "glory." The white sees in the words "free enterprise" and "democracy" unlimited opportunities for the individual who wants to make something of himself. The black perception gives quite different meanings to the same words. Even the word "Christianity" which, through the ages, has represented to the white world the ultimate in ideals—love thy neighbor as thyself—is perceived by blacks as a symbol of repression, an opiate, a philosophy undergirding The System of Enslavement.

The communications experts have discovered that language meaning is not static. The young child who has been bitten by a dog perceives a dog as anything but the lovable, friendly playmate; but, as he grows older, he comes to like dogs. The meaning of language is, therefore, dynamic and constantly changing with the experiences of the perceiver.

"At the heart of our communications problem," says Schwartz, "lies a simple proposition, simple to state, easy to understand, and enormously difficult to accept and use. The idea: words and events do not have meaning—people do." [6]

Further, as Schwartz has pointed out, "When we communicate we are not solely in the news release or reporting business, or the annual report or the meeting business. We are in the people business." [7]

Understanding Students

How well do you really understand the people in your people business—the students? Do you poke fun at them, sneer at their ways, or do you try to understand?

What kind of a society has given meaning to their perceptions? Do you sense their concern over the possibility of an all-out nuclear war? What has the age of plenty, the government handout, and the lack of need to work done to their perceptions? Do you know why they react to The System as they do? How do you, then, get through to them in your communications? And what about Vietnam, the ghetto, riots, and politics—do you see your students in the light of this kind of conditioning? Can you truly put yourself in your students' shoes and know how they feel and think? How often do you get together with your students in an informal way in order to keep yourself tuned in?

Understanding Yourself

How do you see life? How do you see your job? Important? Are you a supporter of or a backbiter at your administration? Are you rigidly authoritarian? Namby-pamby permissive? Just what are you trying to accomplish on your job? How much influence do you think you really have with students? How could you improve?

Understanding Your Communications

Why do you send the kinds of communications you do to students? Do they really affect student behavior? Are the same communications sent to engineering students as to liberal arts students? Why? Are they not motivated quite differently? What is the bulletin board fare like? Run-of-the-mill? How could it be improved? Ever try letting students write your copy and do illustrations for you? What perceptions do the faculty have of placement? What do you do to feed their egos? And how are you helping the administration to understand what you really do, how important your work is? Or is it? How essential are you? Is placement really something more than a bureau of appointments? If some real education is not going on within your office, why not? And if it is, how are you telling that story to your superiors?

Affecting Student Behavior

This is easier said than done. But the Peace Corps in its early years communicated especially well with our youth. Why? Because it put to work the "people have meaning" philosophy. It showed a student how the Corps could become a part of his developing self-concept. It perceived as the students of the day did; hence, it affected responses. Here is a sample of Peace Corps communication taken from one of the Corps' early recruiting pamphlets:

> "When someone asks me (Sargent Shriver speaking), 'What is the Peace Corps?' I begin not with the concept, or the organization, or the program, but with the men and women—they are the Peace Corps . . . they have come with a spirit of determination and idealism . . . I am convinced that faith in democracy, the belief in a civilization based on the dignity of the individual human being, the readiness to sacrifice to enable such a civilization to live and grow, the willingness to serve another person—these are waiting to be topped . . . it is not easy to serve in the Peace Corps for the tests are thorough, the interviews are probing, the training rigorous. . . ." [8]

In another Corps pamphlet the work was described as "requiring the heart of a teacher, the mind of a military technician, the ambition of a poet, the work eagerness of a hungry laborer, and the flexibility of copper wire. All these characteristics must be tempered by exactly the right amounts of humility, creativity, and maturity." [9]

The words of the Peace Corps hit right at the solar plexus of many college students. In these descriptions they saw themselves at their best; they saw their needs being met; they saw their ideals in action; they saw fulfillment. This is the kind of communication that has successfully affected the lives of many college students.

It is no secret, either, that the type of responsibility that the Corps has thrust at once upon its volunteers would take several years, at best, to achieve in the average corporation.

Dynamism would seem to be the clue to understanding both the individual and his perceptions. Because meanings are continuously influenced by changing environmental conditions, perceptions constantly change, and one person's perceived realities are not those of another. This, then, is the challenge of communication: how best to understand behavior and, then, to affect it.

Put yourself in your students' shoes; anticipate how they may respond to your communications. Try to see yourself as a source of communication in the same way that your students see you as that source.

The task is monumental!

BIBLIOGRAPHY

1 Irion, Mary Jean, *From the Ashes of Christianity,* J. B. Lippincott Co., Philadelphia, 1968.

2 Kauffman, Joseph F., *The Student in Higher Education,* The Hagen Foundation, New Haven, Conn., 1968, p. 22.

3 Hughes, Langston, "Ballad of the Landlord."

4 Isaacs, Charles S., "A J.H.S. 271 Teacher Tells It Like He Sees It," *N.Y. Times Magazine,* Nov. 24, 1968, pp. 52 ff.

5 Schwartz, James W., *The Publicity Process,* Iowa State U. Press, 1966, p. 214.

6 Schwartz, James W., ibid., p. 213.

7 Schwartz, James W., ibid., p. 240.

8 Shriver, Sargent, "The Peace Corps," Washintgon, D. C.

9 The Peace Corps, "College Education Plus," p. 5.

CHAPTER 10

Some Legal and Ethical Aspects of Student Personnel Work

THE "NOW GENERATION," TUNED IN and turned on, is at once both the hope and the despair of many college administrators. The aberrations of activist students have shattered well-established but unchallenged patterns of thought and behavior. Yet, is not this what college is all about—a time and place for students to test new ideas as well as their elders and themselves, a place in which to challenge old values, where one can experiment with life styles and develop one's own philosophy? In such an environment, there must inevitably develop both tension and conflict. The problem for the administrator becomes one of how best to relate, in times of stress, to the student.

In Loco Parentis

As has been pointed out in an earlier chapter, there was a time when education dealt with these problems in a highly moralistic, authoritarian fashion. But as educational institutions became more secular they also became more liberal. The moralistic view gave way to the universally accepted practice of establishing the college as a parent surrogate; *in loco parentis* has endured for generations. Under this concept, the college, in its role as parent substitute, made manifest its genuine concern for its children through the establishment of such educational adjuncts as counseling and placement which probably never would have developed had it not been for the parent surrogate view of responsibility. The family of the student, in turn, has, historically, looked upon the college as having a very special obligation to its children; they were to be encouraged, guarded, and protected; obviously, they could not be given the rights and freedoms of the unprotected adult. In short, the student world was set apart from the adult world.

Academia and the Protected Environment

In a somewhat parallel fashion, faculties have also been nurtured in a privileged environment which protects their academic freedom. This freedom, under certain conditions, which vary from one institution to another, establishes an autonomous community which guarantees financial security through tenure. The guarantee further gives a free hand to the tenured to decide who shall gain tenure on the faculty as well as what shall be taught.[1]

In this rarefied environment the student had precious few rights. The time was, and not so long ago, when, upon a faculty member's word, and usually without a hearing, a student could be suspended or dismissed from an educational institution. In effect, the only right the student had was the right to an education.

In Loco Parentis vs. Civil Rights

As a *modus operandi* today, *in loco parentis* is outmoded, passé. The fairly widespread viewpoint is held that "American law probably never imposed a duty, nor conferred a right, on colleges to supervise the general morals of students except where college discipline and educational performance are involved; and if it did, . . . custom and law have changed; and if they have not changed, . . . they ought to . . ." [2]

In recent years the war in Vietnam, the failure of the Congress to concern itself with equitable means of conscription, the civil rights movement, and the tragic assassinations of the Kennedys and Martin Luther King have all been powerful stimulants in developing student activists.

Further, the impersonality of today's industrial society, the bigness of the megalopolis-culture, the remoteness the individual experiences from the centers of political power, and his ineffectiveness in making himself felt by those in power—these and similarly related forces have produced an identity crisis. "What today's protest really represents," says Dean Berg, "is a search for identity, a cry for status and for a feeling of personal worth in today's society." [3] Irving Kristol, vice president of *Basic Books,* puts it this way, "Practically every college student these days understands what is meant by an 'identity crisis'; it is one of the clichés of the Sixties. It is not, perhaps, too much to say that mass picketing on the campus is one of the last twitches of a slowly expiring American individualism." [4] The point is, according to Berg, [3] that students who stone police or who jeer and curse university officials, who carry placards with obscenities on them, or who hold nude parties are really not demanding civil and academic anarchy, more freedom of speech, or an end to all sexual mores. They, rather, insist on being taken notice of.

One popular approach today to the legal rights of students is the civil rights philosophy, a point of view espoused by the American Civil Liberties Union. [5] This holds that the relationship between college and student is contractual and that each party must be "en garde," that constant vigilance is necessary to see to it that contractual responsibilities are adhered to. The civil rights philosophy is primarily interested in the protection of individual differences. Most libertarians would prohibit individual evaluation, either by the professor or any of the student counseling services.

Over the years, counselors and placement educators have been called upon frequently (sometimes by students themselves) to appraise students by evaluating their abilities, interests, and personality qualities. If the civil rights point of view comes to be shared by our courts, the student could bring suit against the placement counselor who violates respect for individual differences. If it could be proved in a lawsuit that failure to be admitted to graduate school or failure to secure a job were due to an uncomplimentary evaluation, a judgment against the counselor might result.

The Law and the University

Within the parameters of the civil rights point of view, what is the legal position of the student counselor? Historically, charitable institutions were considered immune from strikes, garnishment, certain federal taxes, and from civil suits (tort immunity). The tort immunity of public institutions of higher learning was derived from our inheritance of a medieval body of English common law which in effect said, "The king can do no wrong." Under this philosophy of sovereign immunity, the public institution could do no wrong. Private charitable institutions were also exempted from suit by students and employees but on entirely different grounds. A charitable institution is under no liability to the recipients of its benefits (The Trust Fund Doctrine).

This was the posture of the courts for centuries. The record clearly indicates, however, that judicial rulings have applied mainly to state institutions which have been viewed as arms of state governments and, therefore, subject to the same mandates. Few cases have dealt with private colleges. However, in 1942 Associate Justice of the U.S. Court of Appeals for the District of Columbia, Wiley Blount Rutledge, delivered a devastating opinion against the rule of charitable immunity (Georgetown vs. Hughes). The case dealt with an injured employee whose injury was caused by the negligence of another employee in the course of duty. In the opinion of Rutledge, "the incorporated charity should respond as do private individuals, business corporations, and others, when they do good the wrong way." The immunity of charitable institutions became increasingly challenged, so that by 1955 only 12 states were left which recognized the doctrine of complete immunity for charitable institutions.

A more recent chapter in the growing accumulation of case law was written in 1961 (Dixon vs. Alabama State Board of Education). Six students were expelled from Alabama State College without either notice of charges or hearings. They had participated in a sit-down demonstration in a local, publicly owned restaurant. While the District Court upheld the university action, the Court of Appeals reversed the decision with the statement that dismissal without notice of charges or a hearing is unconstitutional.

In writing its decision the court declared that due process must comply with the following standards:

1. The notice to the student should contain a statement of the specific charges and the grounds which, if proved, would justify expulsion.

2. The hearing should include an opportunity to hear both sides in considerable detail and preserve the elements of an adversary proceeding, similar to a trial in a criminal court.

3. The student should be given the names of the witnesses against him and an oral or written report on the facts to which witnesses will testify.

4. The student should be given the opportunity to present his own defense and to produce either oral testimony or written affidavits of witnesses in his behalf.

5. The results of the hearing should be preserved in a report open to the inspection of the student.

In June 1965, Paul Schiff, an activist and editor of a student rights newsletter, *Logos,* was expelled from Michigan State University as a graduate student. Schiff had agitated over discrimination in local housing and was considered by university authorities to be a "disruptive influence." As was the case with the Alabama students, Schiff was given neither notice of charges nor hearing. He took his case to court; the Federal District Court declared the expulsion to be unlawful and ordered the university to give the plaintiff in writing the reasons for expulsion, together with a hearing. The university capitulated; Schiff was allowed to enroll the following term. The Fourteenth Amendment prohibits the states from depriving a citizen of "life, liberty, or property, without due process of the law," and from denying him equal protections of the law. It is this due process which guarantees a student's civil rights.

Until September 1968, there was growing indication of the courts becoming increasingly interested in guaranteeing students' civil rights. However, on September 19, 1968, a startlingly significant decision was handed down by the U.S. District Court for Western Missouri (Scroggin vs. Lincoln University) which upholds the right of a college to set rules and mete out punishment. If this decision becomes a pattern which influences other decisions, it will set a new landmark in student-college legal relationships. This case dealt with the suspension of students who had been involved in violent confrontation with their college (a state university) administration.

The decision sustained the action of university officials in their disciplining of students and, in part, had this to say:

> "If it is true, as it well may be, that man is in a race between education and catastrophe, it is imperative that educational institutions not be limited in the performance of their lawful missions by unwarranted judicial interference.
>
> "Attendance at a tax-supported educational institution of higher learning is . . . optional and voluntary . . . By such voluntary entrance, the

student voluntarily assumes obligations of performance and behavior reasonably imposed by the institution of choice relevant to its lawful missions, processes, and functions.

"These obligations are generally much higher than those imposed on all citizens by the civil and criminal law.

"So long as there is no invidious discrimination, no deprival of due process, no abridgement of a right protected in the circumstances, and no capricious, clearly unreasonable, or unlawful action employed, the institution may discipline students to secure compliance with these higher obligations as a teaching method or to sever the student from the academic community.

"Student discipline is a part of the teaching process except in the case of irrevocable expulsion for misconduct. Even then, the process is not punitive or deterrent in the criminal law sense, but the process is rather the determination that the student is unqualified to continue as a member of the educational community.

"The First Amendment does not prohibit an educational institution from protecting itself against conduct that would destroy it . . . No principle of law requires an educational institution to commence disciplinary proceedings at a time when the campus is in an uproar. Appropriate action can be taken, consistent with the circumstances, to insure the temporary removal of students and others who persist in efforts to reduce the academic community to a state of permanent chaos . . .

"If a particular educational institution has promulgated an appropriate disciplinary code, and is engaged in the process of following such a code, it need not fear that one of its students will be able to maintain some sort of federal court action before the institution has had a reasonable period of time, under the circumstances, within which to conduct a proper disciplinary proceeding in accordance with its established code." [6]

Some educational administrators speculate on just how far the courts may go. Will student protestors so sharply focus the attention of the courts on ambiguous and antiquated student regulations that the courts may become involved in passing judgment on the regulations, or will the pattern established in Scroggin vs. Lincoln University become the law of tomorrow? The thought of the courts becoming involved in the evaluation of university policy is nightmarish to many an educator, for to do so would be a strike at the heart of institutional prerogative.

Developing Positive Relationships With Students

James Penney offers some positive suggestions to student personnel workers who seek to improve student-college relationships. He suggests that, in dealing with students, there be "as little . . . restriction as is reasonably compatible with the maintenance of an operating social order . . . that there be in effect few, if any, restrictions that will not be largely self-enforcing in the hands of men of good will. The natural consequences of failure to comply will be self-evident and thus serve as sufficiently directing in most cases." [7] Penney further urges that relationships be "open to what, in the political realm, have recently been called 'unlimited negotiation,' but which might better be phrased as continuous dialogue in the areas of institutional and individual objectives, rights, freedoms, and responsibilities." [7] Penney believes administrators and faculty "should be alert to possibilities for action rather than pushed to the necessity for reaction. They should be continually seeking new ways and places to teach . . ." [7]

In a similar vein in discussing the student and his relationship to the university, *The Moderator* has this to say, "If the college administration in regulating and disciplining student behavior does not conduct itself towards the student in such a way as to merit his respect, then it has failed in what may be its most significant function . . ." [8]

The Law and the Counselor

Where do the placement educator and the student counselor stand with respect to the law today? In a paper presented before the American College Personnel Association in Minneapolis on April 12, 1965, Justin C. Smith,[9] a professor in the School of Law at Western Reserve University, pointed out four kinds of situations that could give rise to libelous action in the course of student personnel work:

1. any false statement which brings disgrace to the party accused;
2. any statement which falsely accuses a person of a crime of moral turpitude;
3. any statement which falsely accuses a person of want of fitness to conduct his business;
4. any statement falsely accusing a person suffering from a contagious disease.

On the positive side, one may ask what can the student personnel educator do with some degree of impunity? To this Professor Smith replies that the student personnel worker may keep such records as he deems necessary which include academic and non-academic information. He may discuss with employers or other educational institutions such problems as grades, academic failures, dismissal, and the like. Non-academic information such as marital status, race, color, creed, social activities, memberships, social probation, and the like, had best be done on an ad hoc basis. Of course, one must be prudent in giving information about brushes with the law. Information on finances should be held strictly confidential.

There is another aspect of the law which confronts the student counselor: the question of privileged communication. Lawyers, physicians, and ministers share privileged communication status in most states. Must the placement office, for example, reveal information in the student personnel file to prospective employers, governmental agencies, the Armed Forces?

The fact is that there is virtually no case information available on the subject. It is not certain if a counselor might be held in contempt of court if he failed to divulge confidential information. However, this much can be noted: most evidence available to counselors is hearsay. The possession of hearsay evidence that a client violated social convention or a local statute does not make the counselor liable to disclose such information. Counseling problems are basically ethical, not legal.

Because the legal rights of the student counselor are not entirely clear, and because the counselor will be called upon often to evaluate both students and alumni, it is advised that a release statement be procured from the client in advance of making written or verbal evaluations. A typical release statement might read as follows:

> "I hereby authorize XYZ University and its representatives to release to prospective employers, the military services, and educational institutions, information concerning my personal and scholastic qualifications."

Of course, the placement office must abide by fair employment legislation—both state and federal.

Joint Statement on Rights and Freedoms of Students

For some time the American Association of University Professors has been concerned with problems surrounding the academic freedom of students. In June 1967, representatives of the A.A.U.P., the U.S. National Student Association, Association of American Colleges, National Association of Student Personnel Administrators, and the National Association of Women Deans and Counselors, together drafted the Joint Statement on Rights and Freedoms of Students. This statement is found in the Appendix.

Ethics and the Client

The placement educator is primarily concerned with the well-being of his client. While the counselor has loyalties both to his employer and to society as well, the counselee takes precedence at all times. This means that confidential information such as grades, the results of psychological tests, faculty recommendations, and the like, cannot be released without the permission of the client. The counselor will guard client confidences as a trust.

Materials derived from the counselor-client relationship are not to be used for any purpose without the consent of the counselee, or unless the identity of the subject is obscured beyond any chance of recognition.

Since the counselor is already being paid by his college to perform counseling services for the student body, fees or other forms of remuneration cannot be accepted.

In the counselor-counselee relationship, the welfare of the counselee must dictate what may or may not be transmitted to a prospective employer.

Ethics and the Employer Relationship

The placement office is not an employment bureau per se; it is an educational adjunct of the classroom, and if what goes on in the placement office does not have considerable educational value, the office has little justification for existence. Placement offices should aid the student in the developmental tasks of knowing himself, establishing value goals, defining life styles compatible with his goals, and exploring occupations commensurate with his self-concept. The relationship of the placement office to the student is, therefore, basically a counseling relationship.

The placement director must, then, guard against the temptation "to place" clients with potential employers. The counselor may make company materials available; he may accumulate occupational information; he may administer and interpret diagnostic tests; he may help the student to relate his abilities, interests, and personality traits to job needs. But beyond this he cannot—he dare not—go! And this the company had best understand, perquisites notwithstanding.

Principles and Practices

Because of the genuine desire on the part of college placement offices and employers to keep the college-student-employer relationship highly ethical, a code of ethics was first established by the College Placement Council in 1957, revised in 1964, and restructured in 1967.[10] These ethical principles and suggested practices, called *The Principles and Practices of College Recruiting,* are subscribed to by the eight regional placement associations in the United States and Canada. Acceptance of the code, reproduced in the Appendix, is prerequisite to membership in almost all regional associations. It is the placement educator's guide to counselor-student-company relationships.

The ethical implications of counseling are not all black and white, however. There occasionally arise great gray areas when the counselor wonders really where his loyalties lie. In the last analysis, the counselor's conscience must be his guide.

BIBLIOGRAPHY

1 Position paper, "Statement of Faculty Responsibility for the Academic Freedom of Students," AAUP Bulletin, December 1965.

2 Strickland, Donald A., "In Loco Parentis—Legal Mots and Student Morals," *Journal of College Student Personnel,* 1965, Vol. 6, pp. 335 ff.

3 Berg, Irwin A., "What's Really Behind Our Students' Unrest?," College Board Review, No. 60, Summer 1966, p. 11.

4 Kristol, Irving, "What's Bugging the Students," Atlantic, November 1965, p. 108.

5 "Academic Freedom and the Civil Liberties of Students," American Civil Liberties Union, 1961.

6 The Chronicle of Higher Education, October 14, 1968, pp. 1 and 4.

7 Penney, James, "Variations on a Theme: In Loco Parentis," Journal of College Student Personnel, January 1967, pp. 22–25.

8 Hall, Ridgway, "Expulsion and the Student," The Moderator, April 1966, p. 12.

9 Smith, Justin C., unpublished address given at the annual convention of the American Personnel and Guidance Association in Minneapolis, Minnesota on April 12, 1965.

10 Principles and Practices of College Placement and Recruitment, College Placement Council, Inc., Bethlehem, Pa., 1967.

CHAPTER 11

Special Challenges
to Counselors

THERE ARE A NUMBER OF GROUPS in the work force that need the special attention of the placement office: women, black students (and other racial minorities), dropouts, the handicapped (victims of epilepsy, the deaf, the blind, the mute, the palsied, the emotionally disturbed, those severely crippled—to mention a few).

Women

Biological, psychological, economic, and sociological factors combine to complicate the lives of women. The old question, "Marriage *or* career?", heard in earlier generations, has been replaced more often by the question, "Marriage *and* career— how can they best be combined?" There are many reasons why so many modern women aspire to the dual role of raising a family and working. One reason, surely, is economic: the higher cost of living plus the subliminal, and not so subliminal, forces at work on consumers to aspire to ever-higher standards of living.

Labor-saving devices and our "ready-made" economy make marriage *and* careers not only possible but probable. They also create additional leisure time which to many is burdensome. The vegetables are packaged; the cans are easy to open; the clothing is ready-made; housekeeping and cleaning are easy. There is even "baby-sitting" at the local public nursery school. And now, the pill.

The real work motive, however, for an increasing number of college-educated women is for self-realization and self-fulfillment. Women are not only wives and mothers; they are also human beings with talents, interests, and desires not necessarily related to their biological role. Society has increasingly recognized this fact and accepted the consequences of it, reinforced, no doubt, by economic pressures. Some women find adequate fulfillment and satisfaction from developing their talents and interests within the family and in the community through voluntary agencies . . . from the Girl Scouts to the League of Women Voters. Ever more women seek wider roles and greater recognition in business, government, the arts, education, and the social services. They also want the more obvious recognition which the economic system confers by way of a paycheck equal to their male counterparts. Many a "professional volunteer" has been heard to say, en route to the employment office, "If I'm going to work so hard, I might as well get paid for it!" The more highly educated a woman is, the more likely she is to go back into paid employment.

The child-bearing and child-caring activities of women have played a major role in conditioning societal attitudes toward women. Despite legislation, women are not treated as equals to men in many business establishments. They find themselves in lower paying jobs; they tend to be given less challenging jobs; and often they are not given a place on the promotional ladder.

But the American scene *is* changing. In 1870 there were 2 million women in the work force—only 15% of the working population. A century later, however, 35% of the labor force, or approximately 23 million workers, are women; and the number is rapidly increasing. The kinds of jobs they hold have changed radically, too. In 1910 about 42% of the women employed were in unskilled jobs. The fact is that there is a much higher percentage of males than females in unskilled work today. Further, there has been a decided movement of women into both professional and managerial occupations. [1] Some employers, notably government, are respecting the spirit as well as the letter of equal opportunity legislation. Between 1950–1960 there was a 132% increase in the employment of women in recreation, 105% in personnel and labor relations, 104% in medical and dental technology; but there was also a 43% increase in accountants and auditors, and a 42% increase in editors and reporters. [2] Springer calls attention [3] to several other fields in which there is a sharp increase in demand for women college graduates: automotive, marketing, banking and finance, urban development, industrial management, geriatrics, and law enforcement.

As this is being written it seems likely that an additional push toward equality in pay and opportunity will be given as a result of guidelines on sex discrimination prepared by the U.S. Labor Department's Office of Federal Contract Compliance.

The fact that over a third of the work force and nearly one-half of the college population is composed of women does not mean that the placement office will counsel women in exactly the same fashion in which it counsels men. A young woman's orientation toward career choice or toward employment ordinarily differs from that of a young man. While both young men and young women have marriage in view, its effect on the vocational choices and planning of a young woman are necessarily different, even in contemporary society.

Women who work fall roughly in two categories. First there are those women for whom marriage and family will be the predominant factors around which they will organize their lives and work. Then there are those women for whom some sort of career activity will be a psychic necessity and the factor around which life and marriage are organized.

How is a young woman of college age to know which pattern will be hers? If one accepts a developmental theory of vocational choice (indeed it is plain common sense) one must acknowledge that for most it is impossible to choose or know absolutely. Nevertheless, some preliminary assumptions may be valuable and necessary.

One of the most important tasks of a counselor working with young women is to challenge them to think seriously about the world of work in the light of their own values, interests, talents, and purposes. It is important that a young woman realize, in view of contemporary trends, that she will spend a substantial part of her life in paid employment. (Indeed, current statistics show that 70–80% of women college graduates are in the work force.) This is true even if she believes herself to be one of those, still clearly in the majority, for whom job experience will have a varying degree of importance, ranging from negligible to very substantial, but who quite clearly intends to accept the fact that marriage and especially children may limit, interrupt, or give a special shape to her working life. It would seem obvious, then, that the counseling of such women, in the light of trends, needs to be oriented in three directions—(1) pre-marriage, (2) early marriage, and (3) post-child-rearing employment at an increasingly early age. How will she make the best use of her talents in a pre-marriage job? Can pre-marriage employment provide a good career beginning in the event that marriage plans do not develop as expected? How can she capitalize on that job experience during the early years of her marriage? (Indeed, many young women start in at both marriage and a job at the same time.) How, with intelligent planning, can these initial work experiences plus, perhaps, part-time study or work lead into satisfying post-child-rearing employment? How can serious volunteer activity open new career possibilities or develop old ones?

However, there will be some young women who have reached a firm decision that they belong to the group for whom a career is essential, who will find personal satisfaction and fulfillment only through a strong commitment to a profession or to work that provides opportunity for real career development. Such a woman will still have marriage in view. A young woman in this category is likely to need special understanding, encouragement, and reinforcement. She will face on occasion a barrage of discouragement, disbelief, or even ridicule from friends or acquaintances, older and younger, male and female. She may even face opposition from family members whose values differ from her own. She will need to be aware of possibly difficult choices ahead.

In connection with marriage she will be faced with the need to choose a husband whose values are compatible with her own. She will need to accept the fact that, when there is competition with men for advancement she will have to prove her own commitment and seriousness of purpose time and again whereas it will be assumed in the case of her male counterparts. She will need to be prepared to act on the principle that many doors will not be opened unless she knocks on them vigorously. Just as her male classmates, she must often make her plans for professional education early, as in the case of medicine. Career counselors should be as alert to the fact that some young women need to be sought out and provided with requisite information as they are to the needs of their men students. Successful career women should be brought back for career conferences as well as successful career men.

If the placement office offers services to alumnae, those women whose working careers have been interrupted may well need special counseling in relation to the opportunities open to them when they are ready again to seek employment. There will be new fields of which they are unaware. Some of them will have suffered loss of confidence and sense of self as a result of years spent identified chiefly as someone's mother or someone's wife. They may be unaware of the potential values in the experiences and skills gained in community organizations and volunteer activities.

Those who have worked with women returnees, or would-be returnees to the labor market, have discovered that there are special problems and considerations for the counselor to have in mind. In a number of institutions where continuing education programs have developed, special counselors have been provided, working often with both men and women. There is, or should be, close coordination and cooperation with the placement office in such instances.

Although these points are far from giving adequate coverage to the subject, they will at least suggest that the counseling of women at the college level becomes a more complicated problem than the counseling of men. In many cases the real challenge to the counselor—male or female—may be not to impose his own bias and his own personal view of the role of a woman in society on the women to whom he is giving assistance. Is he limiting the horizons they should explore? Or is he helping to develop among women the knowledge that they have choices; that there are opportunities in fields not thought of, traditionally, as female; that when they have made their choices there is sympathy and support for their endeavors?

The Minority Group Student

The fact that one belongs to a minority group has had a severely limiting effect upon vocational choice. Usually, when minority group problems are mentioned, one automatically thinks of blacks because they constitute the largest minority group. But the problems encountered by American Indians, Orientals, and Puerto Ricans are just as real.

It has been well over a decade since the famous 1954 Supreme Court decision (Brown vs. Board of Education) decreed that "separate" meant "unequal." Yet, how much progress has been made in opening the doors of higher education to black students? In a recent study of programs for the disadvantaged in colleges in the northeastern United States—an area which prides itself on its lack of discrimination—Kendrick reports in the *College Board Review* [4] that "in all colleges of all kinds in the region (in 1965–66) sixty-nine one-hundredths of one per cent (0.69%) of the students were Negro . . ."

An appreciation of the national picture can be obtained from a U.S. Department of Health, Education, and Welfare publication entitled *Undergraduate Enrollment by Ethnic Group in Federally-Funded Institutions of Higher Education*.[5] The data are for 1968, the most recent year studied. HEW reported that 6.0% of the total enrollment was Negro; 0.6% American Indian; 1.0% Oriental, and 1.9% Spanish-surnamed.

This kind of record is convincing evidence to minority groups (and an increasing number of white liberals) that the United States is institutionally racist. Blacks, out of their frustrations, believe that any white-black coalition is a myth, and they very much resent any white paternalistic approach to a solution of the problem.

In one way the black student in the black college may wind up with fewer problems in vocational counseling than the black in a white college. In most non-black institutions, both the black student and the white counselor face an almost insurmountable hurdle. The color of their respective skins makes for a tremendous credibility gap. Blacks just don't believe whites. Perhaps the first step to understanding is for the white counselor to admit that he can't possibly understand the black's problems, no matter how hard he tries. Some progress may be made by white counselors with black students who have had most of their pre-college education in predominantly white schools; probably not so with graduates of ghetto schools.

Kenneth S. Washington, assistant to the chancellor at the University of California at Los Angeles, discusses this problem at the secondary school level. What he says obviously applies at the college level, too. "Every (white) counselor has several handicaps in his attempts to relate to young (black) students. He is an adult and this often makes communication stem from entirely different worlds. He is an employee of the school system and is, thus, suspect. He is committed to education and is, thus, seen to have a bias . . . The racial difference between the counselor and the student, coupled with Black Power's reluctance to discuss conflicts outside of the family, makes the task more difficult and more challenging—but not impossible . . . Counselors must learn the language patterns of black students so that true meanings are communicated . . ." [6] (For an attempt at language understanding of black by white, see bibliography, reference number 7.) The real problem, then, with the black student is how the white counselor can possibly relate to the black, or the black to the white. Once this relationship can be established, the rest is comparatively easy. There are many more jobs available to blacks in business, government, education, and the professions than there are blacks who are qualified to take the jobs.

One of the best ways to develop understanding, and to inspire the confidence of blacks, according to such organizations as CORE, NAACP, and the Urban League, is to add black counselors to the staff. If a college is small, has a genuine interest in working with blacks but cannot employ a full-time black counselor, the college might hire blacks who can work in other areas of the college, in addition to placement.

Whatever the approaches to the minority student problems, these groups will need more time and attention than the run-of-the-mill student. Expect the black to be alienated and hostile, and know why. Know why he believes the 1954 United States Supreme Court decision, the 1960 nationwide civil rights demonstrations, the great march on Washington in 1963, and the 1964 "long hot summer" in Mississippi were all failures. Do some serious reading. As a starter, and probably a shocker, try Eldridge Cleaver's *Soul on Ice*.[8] The book will compel attention by both the beauty and terrifying lucidity of the author's prose.

Before white student personnel workers can ever relate to blacks, the whites must see that concessions made in the name of civil rights have only further aggravated blacks who believe that the nation has in no way, as yet, begun to meet the needs of the black millions locked into economic deprivation.

This will be the toughest, most frustrating, yet the most necessary job the placement counselor has yet had to do.

The Handicapped

The deaf, the blind, the palsied, the crippled, the epileptic, the emotionally disabled, and other handicapped college students generally create serious placement problems for the placement office.

The number of handicapped who need employment is quite apt to increase for some very logical reasons. Modern medicine has found ways to control the epileptic seizure and the diabetic coma; in short, the life span of the handicapped group is constantly being increased. Furthermore, since competition for employment is a pretty fierce problem for the handicapped, the more education he has the better; hence the number of college-educated handicapped is increasing all the time.

Companies often tend to throw out a variety of reasons why they cannot hire the handicapped: (1) they are not reliable; (2) they will put a severe strain on sick benefit and group insurance plans; (3) they are not very flexible and cannot, therefore, be moved from one job to another; (4) they have a high rate of absenteeism; (5) they require special advantages; (6) the disabled are not as efficient as other workers; (7) other workers do not want to work with the handicapped; (8) they cannot pass the physical examination, anyway.

Several studies reveal typical employer attitudes toward the disabled. Grob and Olshansky, for example, in a study covering 90,000 workers and 200 employers in Greater Boston, found that while about 75% of the employers said they would hire employees with previous emotional disturbances, only 27 of the 200 employers had knowingly hired such personnel, and, interestingly, 4 of the 200 employers accounted for better than 25% of the 58 hired.[9] This is typical of the kind of problem that confronts the placement offices: what the employer says he will do, and what he actually does in the hiring of the handicapped, are often poles apart.

An attitudinal study of 306 supervisors in the Minneapolis–

St. Paul area found that while companies agreed that they would hire handicapped workers who are willing to work hard, opportunities for advancement were few; and, in fact, a very limited number of jobs in each of the companies was believed suitable for the handicapped.[10]

Borow[11] refers to a three-year study in New York City of seven major industries in the hiring of individuals with cardiac impairment, orthopedic conditions, epilepsy, cerebral palsy, and serious vision problems; 436 companies participated in the study (199 large corporations, 174 moderate size and 63 small companies). Only 37% of the large and moderate-size companies and 22% of the small companies had knowingly hired disabled employees. There is abundant evidence of considerable discrimination against the handicapped, many of whom are quite as able to perform as well on a job as the non-handicapped.

How, then, does one counsel the disabled? In the past the handicapped have been stereotyped into jobs. For example, the paraplegic becomes the accountant, the female blind becomes the dictaphone typist, and the orthopedically disabled becomes the watchmaker. Undoubtedly these jobs gave many handicapped employment, but they limited what the handicapped might do. Certainly it is a fact that the disabled may perform successfully in any kind of employment in which their disabilities are not limiting factors.

The counselor of tomorrow's handicapped needs to be far more creative in his counseling. He needs to know well the gamut of occupational information and how to relate the assets of the handicapped to that information. Too often past counsel has overemphasized the negative; it has dwelt too patronizingly on the handicap. It is important, rather, to accentuate the positive, for the facts are that the physically handicapped and normal employees both have similar production, job turnover, accident, and absentee records.

The placement director will often have to turn on his most persuasive arguments with prospective employers, which indeed he should do, in order to bring about both understanding and action on the part of employers. It will be necessary to parry employer arguments about absenteeism, reliability, efficiency, physical stamina—ad infinitum—with the power of informed persuasion about the handicapped; namely, that the disabled are quite capable of holding their own. They ask no favors; they simply want an opportunity to prove themselves. As more handicapped are employed, their job performance will bear testimony to their abilities and the task of counseling and placement will become less arduous.

The Dropout

Nearly 50% of all students who enter college leave with no degrees. This indicates the magnitude of the dropout problem. A variety of causes produces the dropout: financial problems, poor scholastic achievement, poorly defined goals, marriage, and the need to go to work—to mention a few. However, an increasing number of individuals become attrition statistics because of emotional difficulties. At the source of many a problem is stress—stress produced by the sheer numbers of students and the consequent impersonality of the techniques used to cope with the numbers problem.

The National Student Association at a special workshop in 1965 considered the causes of student stress. Three major areas of stress were defined: (1) the contradiction between the standards of excellence and the actual practices in colleges; (2) the intensity and rigidity of the academic program; (3) problems of relating to the relevant social world.[12]

To illustrate: the entering student has read in the college catalogue all about excellence, and how the purpose of college is to learn how to think and be able to solve problems. He goes to his first class; the professor stresses independence of thought and urges student skepticism. But then comes a first examination, and what does the student find but a number of questions requiring the memorization of a large body of discrete facts. The message comes through loud and clear that memorization will earn an A; creative thinking is for the birds. The story is told of one student who dropped out of college "because he was succeeding and suddenly realized that he did not believe in what he was doing." [13] Dialogue with almost any group of students will supply one with an endless supply of similar cases.

The fact is that college administrations and faculties through sheer neglect of student reactions and student attitudes unwittingly have created violently stressful situations. Dr. Benson Snyder, psychiatrist-in-chief at M.I.T., has this to say about student stress: "(Student) failure, his distress, his stress, is, in some measure, our failure, our distress, our stress . . . A dialogue is overdue." [14]

Since the college is the source of the stress in a great many situations, and, therefore, a major cause in the development of a dropout, the college has a responsibility to develop solutions to alleviate the stress. Certainly, the potential dropout as well as the dropout will need more than average counseling.

From an employment point of view, the dropout is confronted by the myth that dropouts are life-long failures. Many employers tend to subscribe to this myth. It should be a responsibility of the placement office to help explode the myth. The dropout deserves not as much help as the next fellow; he needs much more!

BIBLIOGRAPHY

1 Barry, Ruth and Wolf, Beverly, "Epitaph for Vocational Guidance," Bureau of Publications, Teachers College, Columbia University, New York, 1962, pp. 128–129.

2 United States Bureau of Census, 1960.

3 Springer, Mildred S., "Special Outlook, Special Challenge," *The College Placement Annual*—1969, Bethlehem, Pennsylvania, pp. 30–31.

4 Kendrick, S. A., "The Coming Segregation of Our Selective Colleges," *College Board Review*, Winter 1967–68, pp. 6 ff.

5 *Undergraduate Enrollment by Ethnic Group in Federally-Funded Institutions of Higher Education*, Fall 1968, U. S. Department of Health, Education, and Welfare.

6 Washington, Kenneth S., "What Counselors Must Know About Black Power," *Personnel and Guidance Journal*, November 1968, p. 207.

7 Burke, Carl F., *God Is For Real, Man*, Association Press, New York, 1966.

8 Cleaver, Eldridge, *Soul on Ice*, McGraw-Hill Book Co., New York, 1968.

9 Olshansky, S., "Employer Receptivity," in *Rehabilitation of the Mentally*

Ill, American Association for the Advancement of Science, Washington, D. C., 1959, pp. 213 ff.

[10] Minnesota Studies in Vocational Rehabilitation: IX, "Attitudinal Barriers to Employment," Bulletin 32, Industrial Relations Center, University of Minnesota, Minneapolis, June 1961.

[11] Borow, Henry, *Man in a World at Work,* Houghton Mifflin Co., Boston, 1964, p. 547.

[12] Dennis, Lawrence E., and Kauffman, Joseph F., *The College and the Student,* Am. Council on Education, 1966, p. 343.

[13] Ibid., p. 344.

[14] Ibid., p. 353.

CHAPTER 12

The Junior College
and Placement

WITH WELL OVER A MILLION students enrolled in more than 800 junior colleges in 49 of the 50 states, the junior college is a most important force in higher education today. Most of the junior colleges are coeducational; many are private, but the public sector is growing rapidly. Some have enrollments of a few hundred; others are as large as 10,000 students. Some are comprehensive community colleges offering a potpourri of programs, while others are specialized technical and pre-professional institutions.[1]

The Junior College Student

There is abundant evidence that the more highly motivated high school student with strong scholastic ability and a good achievement record goes to the senior college, whereas the less highly motivated, more practically oriented, student chooses junior college.[2] Perhaps a continuing lack of motivation may be responsible for the low rate of transfer to senior colleges. It is said that "while 75 per cent of the students entering junior college indicate they will transfer to four-year colleges, only 20–30 per cent actually do so." [3]

A study of six junior colleges in the Midwest and California revealed that two-thirds of the students came from families whose occupations demanded special skills but no college degree. In this particular sample, 70 per cent of the women were from non-college homes, and a large proportion of those were taking secretarial and office practice programs; 86 per cent of the students in this study terminated their education either at the end or during the program.[4]

In general, junior college students may be described as individuals who have not yet developed strong motivation, who are not too inclined academically, who are interested in practical things, and who are "likely to be cautious and controlled . . . not sufficiently sure of themselves to explore new and untried fields . . ." but rather "seek more certain pathways to success and financial security." [5, 6]

One of the problems in junior college student personnel work is the lack of objective, reliable, and statistically valid information which will describe the uniqueness of the junior college student. A great deal of work needs to be done here.

The Problems of Stereotyping

In the opinion of Cross:

"The very lack of ability to describe statistically the uniqueness of junior college students indicates the failure of the junior colleges to relate to their students. Still working within the confines of traditional education, junior colleges encourage their students with a weak senior college prescription instead of developing vital, ability-related programs. The result is a high rate of dropouts and a situation where graduates mislocate themselves vocationally, both in terms of preference and ability, and do not attain either the desired job level or the desired proficiency." [5]

Heavy criticism is leveled at junior colleges by some senior college faculties. Especially annoyed are some university department heads over the junior college's "college parallel" programs. The university professor asks, "Parallel to what?" Perel and Vairo ask, "If the community college faculty and administration both lack experience with college courses, how can they tell if the courses which they offer are the proper sort for freshmen and sophomores in college to be taking?" [7] These educators plead for a variety of informal contacts between junior and senior college personnel in order to build a better understanding of one another.

As one reads the literature and talks with teachers and students about the junior college, it would seem that the junior college suffers from being stereotyped: those who can, go to senior colleges; those who cannot, go to junior colleges. All of the criticisms that apply to junior colleges apply as readily to senior colleges. While there are many junior colleges that are weak academically, there are also large numbers of senior colleges with the same problem. An increasing number of the newer junior colleges offer a range and quality of student personnel services, including placement, that puts to shame the student personnel programs in many of our top senior colleges.

The Junior Colleges Rate Themselves

In 1965 the Committee on Appraisal and Development of Junior College Student Personnel Programs, supported by a grant from the Carnegie Corporation, completed the evaluation of junior college student personnel programs in 49 junior colleges with enrollments in excess of 1,000 students and 74 junior colleges with lesser enrollments. [8] The study concluded that the junior colleges, in general, are doing a poor job in their student personnel functions. While junior college catalogues talk a good deal about being "student centered" and giving "individual assistance in personal, educational, and vocational exploration," their deeds in terms of supporting student personnel services were found wanting. One might ask, however, "Is this not a problem which plagues, also, the senior college?"

In the rating of 49 large junior colleges in the Carnegie study, slightly over 10 per cent were rated as "excellent" in student counseling services, whereas nearly 60 per cent were rated as "mediocre," "poor," or "very poor." In placement services, less than 10 per cent were rated as "excellent," and approximately 70 per cent were rated as "mediocre," "poor," or "very poor." Placement activities came very near the bottom of the list of student personnel services in effectiveness of function.[9]

Career Counseling and Placement

Since approximately 75 per cent of the junior college graduates are terminal, there is urgent need for effective career counseling and placement services. This need is further enhanced by the backgrounds of the junior college students. Students who come from non-college families, or whose parents work at non-professional, semi-skilled, and skilled occupations, often have distorted perceptions of reality. There is a tendency to look at education as a means to an end, simply as a tool to a bigger pocketbook or as a vehicle to give greater social status and prestige.

Because vocational choice is a process—developmental—and not a decision in point of time, and because the junior college student is being asked at an earlier age than the senior college graduate to make a commitment, the whole question of placement readiness is involved. Has the junior college student developed and matured to a point of vocational decision? Can the junior college, in fact, give effective help in placement, even if it tries? The answer is not really known.

However, the fact of the matter is that most junior college students are terminal and that they do go to work at the end of two years of college. It can be argued, therefore, that the counseling and placement needs of the junior college student are more urgent than those of the senior college student. Satisfying those needs effectively will be remarkably difficult because of the younger chronological age of the junior college student, compared with his senior college counterpart.

The Junior College Placement Office

All that has been said in Chapters 4, 5, and 6 about placement office services, organization, and facility patterns, and the vocational library can be applied to the junior college. The one difference is that, because the junior college has the student but two years, there is a sense of urgency about counseling and placement. It must get going at once in the freshman year and function intensively.

The American Association of Junior Colleges makes available to its membership an excellent manual on the organization and operation of a junior college placement office: *Service Through Placement in the Junior College.* This publication should be a part of every junior college placement library.

Some junior college administrators have suggested that their placement needs can best be met by the United States Employment Service. Placement should be the end product of an on-campus counseling program, which is not the province of USES. The United States Employment Service, on the other hand, does have good employer contacts and up-to-the-minute job information. Generally speaking, however, most knowledgeable educators believe that each college should maintain its own placement office.

Recruiting at the Junior College

A study of 1,000 full-time placements of a large community college found that 85 per cent were in such areas as office work, technical assistants, merchandising, and semi-professional jobs such as nursing and dental assistants.[10] It is suspected that many employers might do better to recruit for many job openings on junior college campuses rather than on the senior college campus. There has been the tendency to hire engineers when technicians could have done the job, to subject the ambitious four-year graduate to the frustrations of certain kinds of sales jobs which the junior college graduate could do equally well, perhaps even better.

It would seem, then, that with the tremendous labor potential available at the junior colleges, and with the very rapid increase in numbers of two-year graduates, employers in their own interest cannot fail to learn how best to relate to the junior college.

A Look at the Future

To date the junior college has nowhere near begun to meet a national need with which it is eminently qualified to deal. The demand for a great variety of technicians in our economy is practically insatiable. For example, the number of such workers in the U.S. labor force rose from 200,000 in 1950 to 480,000 in 1960—an increase of 140 per cent. According to the U.S. Department of Labor, this need will continue to escalate. Hence, instead of emulating the senior college curriculum, the junior college of tomorrow will find unlimited opportunities for innovation in producing technicians for police work, traffic management, sanitation, fire fighting, food service, pollution technology, sales, data processing, recreation, drafting, library work, cosmetology, photography, drama (broadcasting), television, commercial art and illustration, technical writing, and dental hygiene—to mention a few.

And when such areas of opportunity are made available to the great untapped human potential of the ghetto, the future of the junior college becomes explosive with excitement.

BIBLIOGRAPHY

1 Collins, Charles C., *Junior College Student Personnel Programs—What They Are and What They Should Be*, American Association of Junior Colleges, Washington, D. C., 1967 (a Carnegie Corporation research study), p. 12.

2 Smith, N. A. and Lyon, M. E., "High School Seniors: A Junior College or a Four-Year College?" *Journal College Student Personnel*, March 1968, pp. 105–108.

3 Simon, Lora S., "Counseling the Inappropriately Committed in a Community College," APGA 1968 Detroit Convention Abstracts, p. 252.

4 Hakanson, John W., "Selected Characteristics, Socioeconomic Status, and Levels of Attainment of Students in Public Junior College Occupation-Centered Education," ERIC Report, Ed. 013644, U.S. Office of Education, April 1967, pp. 28 ff.

5 Cross, Patricia K., *The Junior College Student: A Research Description*, Educational Testing Service, Princeton, N.J., 1968, pp. 56 ff.

6 Collins, Charles C., op. cit., p. 12.

7 Perel, W. M. and Vairo, Philip D., "The Community College and the College Parallel Program," *The Journal of Higher Education*, January 1969, pp. 48–49.

8 Collins, Charles C., op. cit., p. 17.

9 Ibid., p. 21.

10 Mohs, Milton C., *Service Through Placement in the Junior College*, American Association of Junior Colleges, Washington, D.C., 1962, p. 8.

CHAPTER 13

The Campus Interview—
A Vital Learning Experience
for Student and Employer

A GREAT DEAL OF CONTROVERSY has been generated in recent years by critics, both students and faculty, who see
the placement office only as an arm of the business establishment. Henry Steele Commager has said:

> "The basic principle which should govern the rela-
> tions of the university to recruiters is that which
> should govern all other activities of the academy.
> The university is not an employment agency; it is
> not an adjunct of corporations; it is not an in-
> strument of government. Wherever feasible, the
> university should make available its facilities to
> legitimate educational enterprises. It is under no
> obligation, whatsoever, to make its facilities avail-
> able to what is not educational." [1]

The Placement Office—an Employment Agency?

In light of the mission of the placement office as set forth in the preceding chapters of this text, Commager is right *if* the main thrust of placement is simply to serve as a bureau of appointments, a meeting place for student job-hunters and employers. But this is *not* the mission of placement today.

The development of the whole individual is the primary aim of higher education. This wholeness implies something far beyond the classroom. It means education for life, and a very real part of living in our industrial society is earning a living. Altogether too many college professors use the words "business" and "industry" as if they were dirty words. To think about how one might apply one's education to earning a living in anything but education or research appears to many a professor to be degrading, to say the least.

There is evidence, particularly on some liberal arts campuses, of the lack of readiness of many college seniors to face the outside world.[2]

Some studies suggest that college students choose work not on the basis of what they have learned about the demands of an occupation but, rather unrealistically, on the imagined life styles of workers.[3]

The placement office, through career counseling, occupational information, by helping the student secure part-time and summer employment, and through the employer campus interview program, can help students put their classroom learnings into realistic perspective. And since there are few students today who can afford the luxury of graduating into the life style of country gentlemen, sooner or later they must go to work. It is both as logical and as important for the college to maintain a placement office with its various services—including the educational experience of employment interviewing—as it is to maintain the college library, bookstore, dining halls, or for that matter fraternities, athletics, and the vast extra-curricular activities program.

It is not an uncommon experience of students to find that extra classroom activities in college have prepared them far better for certain life situations than some classroom learnings. For example, the debating society, the campus newspaper, the fraternity, the theater guild, have developed the ability in individuals to express themselves, to solve problems, to lead. The campus interview brings into play a variety of such learning situations. For example, the student must begin to analyze himself, to know his strengths and weaknesses, and where and how he might apply his talents with some degree of success. For the first time in his life, perhaps, he submits to a process wherein he is being judged as a total personality, and he begins to learn how important it is to know himself and to be able to sell himself. He begins to learn about the world of work, what opportunities are open to him, the paths others have taken to success, and how he might succeed. Here at last, in confrontation with the recruiter, is the challenge to bring into play all he has learned.

The individual who attacks placement and the campus interview as having no value educationally just does not know what placement is all about. Granted, there are good placement offices, and there are poor placement offices. But, then, some history professors are better than others, too.

The Goals of College Recruitment

The college recruiter's reputation with his company is only as good as the college recruits he is able to produce. Company executives, personnel managers, and recruiters seldom admit that college recruitment is essentially a selling job; it cannot be otherwise and succeed. The recruiter's ability to merchandise his company successfully to college students is absolutely essential, but this is only half the task. The recruiter must also be a judge of people. He must be able, through the initial campus interview, to find those individuals whom he believes will make good employees for his company.

Aid from the college placement office in helping the recruiter achieve his goal is essential if a long-term working relationship is to develop. The college may be certain that, if year after year passes and no recruits are forthcoming, the company will abandon its recruitment at that college. The company has no other choice, recruitment costs being what they are. It can be seen, then, that the establishment of productive college-employer relationships are mutually advantageous. How, then, can the college be helpful to the employer?

The Role of the College in Employer Recruitment

If one concedes that it is as important to "know thyself" as it is to know the world around one, then there is limitless educational value in learning how one might relate oneself to the world of work; how one might use what has been learned in gainful employment. A great many educators believe there is value in such mental exercise. Hence, the campus interview program can readily be justified.

In such a context, the concerned placement educator wants to develop as wide a range of interview learning situations as possible. This means the careful development of a broad list of employers that have the kinds of job opportunities that relate to the interests and backgrounds of the particular student body.

Since the employer campus visit is of such short duration, the college needs to make the most of the opportunity. To give students the maximum opportunity to learn from interview experiences, company interview schedules must be publicized well in advance, and with faculty and staff as well as with students. The kind of information to be publicized might well include such data as the name of the employer, date of interviews, positions available, qualifications sought in interviewees, geographical locations of jobs available, names of interviewers, etc. There is need to communicate such information to all of the campus media: radio, TV, bulletin boards, campus newspaper, department heads, etc.

Before the recruiter arrives on campus, if the interviewing is to run smoothly, a carefully developed interview schedule should be prepared. Interviewees should be informed of time and place of interview and name of interviewer and, as part of the learning process, should be reminded that the cardinal sin of an interviewee is taking on an interview without knowing well both himself and the employer who is about to interview him. Here is where the company library really comes into play. After the recruiter arrives, considerable attention must be paid to keeping the interviewer as well as the interviewees on schedule. Adequate time should be worked into the schedule for rest periods and lunch, and faculty members important to the interviewer should be scheduled to join the placement table at lunch.

The Art of Choosing People

There are almost as many theories on the selection of human talent as there are individuals doing the selecting. Twenty-five years ago, the late Paul Boynton [4] greatly influenced campus personnel selection procedures. He suggested that if recruiters would get answers to the following questions, then they would be able to make reasoned judgments about the interviewee:

1. What influenced the interviewee to go to college?
2. Why did he decide on a particular course of study?
3. Why did he select his particular college?
4. Childhood interests?
5. Childhood money-making ventures?
6. Extra-curricular activities?
7. Quality of classroom work?
8. Summer activities?
9. Percentage of college expenses earned?
10. Plans for ultimate career?
11. Philosophy of life?
12. Community interests?

Dr. Robert N. McMurry [5] advocated a simple and workable selection procedure. He maintained that it is relatively easy to measure in a patterned interview a person's "can-do" traits:

appearance and manner, availability, intelligence, experience, skills, and knowledge. However, McMurry pointed out that it is quite another thing to be able to determine what a person "will do" on the job. What he will do will depend on such basic character traits as stability, industry, perseverance, and loyalty. The key to what a man will do is found in what he has done in his schooling, military service, on the job, with his family situation, and by his financial condition. In short, what is really being sought in the interview is an evaluation of the candidate's motivation.

A few years ago Richard A. Fear, then president of the Psychological Corporation, set forth his techniques for predicting job performance through the evaluative interview.[6] Fear advocated a structured interview for the purpose of getting and interpreting information about the candidate—not unlike McMurry's patterned interview. Fear's Interview Guide is reproduced in the Appendix. Here, again, it becomes apparent that the elusive trait sought in the interview is a measure of how highly motivated the candidate is.

The fact remains, as Gellerman well points out, that selection at best "is always a guessing game." [7] Gellerman is a good tonic for every recruiter who takes himself too seriously, playing the role of god in judgment of people. Gellerman warns of a variety of fallacies to which employment managers succumb: the "hero fallacy," the "descriptive fallacy," the "permanence fallacy," and the "fallacy of determinism." [8]

The idea that somewhere someone has just the proper qualifications to meet particular job demands is the hero fallacy. There just is not such a person. Some personnel workers subscribe to the notion that if the job to be filled can be defined accurately, then accurate appraisal of the candidate can bring the two together; all one has to do is find him—fallacy No. 2! The permanence fallacy assumes that once a man has been evaluated, one knows for all time what he needs to know about the candidate. Gellerman points out that this is why so few individuals are re-evaluated in most organizations, and why some organizations have such serious morale problems. Finally, the fallacy of determinism is the notion that an individual's success or failure in a job can be predicted by the presence or absence of particular traits and qualities. It just is not so!

Gellerman very substantially deflates those personnel workers who are sure they have the solution to selection. His discussion of motivational theory in tune with the times suggests that while external awards attract a man to a particular employer, it is the internal rewards that take a man into a particular vocation. If this be so, then the college recruiter of graduating seniors and raw recruits just out of graduate school will want to examine ever so carefully the candidate vis-à-vis the internal reward system.

How Can Placement Help in Selection?

There will be all kinds of recruiters; some will know all the answers; others will not be so certain. All will be looking for a variety of information to interpret as they will in their decision-making. All will be searching for a measure of that elusive thing called motivation. How much help can or should the placement office give in this evaluation procedure?

A great many placement educators refuse to play god. And perhaps this is as it should be. As long as the information which the placement office gives the recruiter is factual and objective, and violates no ethical considerations, then the procedure is acceptable. For example, the knowledge that a student generally receives low grades in areas mathematical and high grades in areas verbal, indicates something worth knowing about a person. The fact that a student is married, works 20 hours a week, and yet maintains high grades must tell something about motivation. It is just as useful to know that the interviewee who just squeaks by academically is a social wheel on campus, the one who can make student events really go.

Certainly the placement educator can play a very important role in helping to evaluate interviewees, short of playing god. The kind and amount of information given will depend a great deal on the philosophy and orientation of the placement educator. Of course, he must remain objective and unbiased.

How the Placement Office Can Blight the Campus Interview Program

Wallace Jamie has called attention to a study made of leading companies in four big industries to find out why they failed to return for interviews on certain campuses. Among the reasons given are the following:

1. "Including persons on my schedule who do not meet the general specifications of age, marital status, and academic qualifications furnished by me prior to the campus visit.
2. "Failure to see that persons coming in for interviews have the opportunity to read descriptive material furnished by me for that purpose. We expressly request that this opportunity be given since it saves valuable time that can be used to better advantage in finding out about the individual rather than spending it in repeating information that is contained in the descriptive material.
3. "Failure to set up the interview schedule on prescribed time limits. For my particular openings and for the type of interview I conduct, I request a half-hour schedule with a minimum of 20 minutes. A 10- or 15-minute schedule is useless to me.
4. "Failure to provide a private space for interviewing. Interviewing in hallways, sharing rooms with representatives of other companies, or interviewing in offices where people are working makes a visit useless. The space does not have to be large or the furnishings luxurious—just private, that's all I ask.

5. "Running campus 'big wheels' through the schedule to give us a treat, especially when these men tell us that they plan to go to graduate school or into professional athletics.

6. "Cramming the schedule with the hard-to-place members of a class in the hope that we will slip and hire one or that at least these students will gain experience from these interviews. One or two of these are all right, but when half the schedule is so taken up, I consider it an imposition.

7. "Posting the notice of my visit on the bulletin board the day of my visit, with no other effort to line up people for my schedule." [9]

It must be apparent to the knowledgeable educator that employer campus interviews are of considerable educational value when they come as the end result of the counseling process. The placement office, more than any other campus service, is able to help the student to help himself by giving the perspective of realism to his educational experience.

BIBLIOGRAPHY

[1] Commager, Henry Steele, "The University as Employment Agency," *The New Republic*, February 24, 1968, pp. 23–26.

[2] Sanford, Nevitt, *Where Colleges Fail*, Jossey-Bass Inc., San Francisco, 1967, p. 186.

[3] Beardslee, D. and O'Dowd, D., "Students and the Occupational World," an unpublished lecture given at Harvard University.

[4] Boynton, Paul W., *Selecting the New Employee*, Harper & Brothers, New York, 1949, pp. 49 ff.

[5] McMurry, Robert N., Dartnell Training Conference brochure, "Personnel Selection."

[6] Fear, Richard A., *The Evaluation Interview*, McGraw-Hill Book Co., Inc., New York, 1958.

[7] Gellerman, Saul W., *Management by Motivation*, American Management Association, Inc., 1968, p. 60.

[8] Gellerman, ibid., pp. 79 ff.

[9] Jamie, Wallace, reprint of a serialized presentation in the *Journal of College Placement*—"A Model Program for Corporate Recruitment of Collegiate Personnel," 1957.

CHAPTER 14

Professional Associations

G UIDANCE, COUNSELING, AND CAREER PLANNING are essential to the guiding of human development. Whatever his role, each type of counselor needs to identify both with his field of specialization in counseling and with counselors in general, so that common learnings and concerns may be shared. Several professional associations are available to the placement educator which can aid him in his professional growth: the Regional Placement Associations, the College Placement Council, and the American College Personnel Association.

The Regional Placement Associations

Prior to World War II, a limited number of colleges had placement offices, and very few employers had well-defined programs of college recruiting. Since World War II, college placement and employer recruitment activities have had phenomenal growth. The question may be asked why it is that the regional placement associations have not become a single national organization? Wisely, this is a move which has been avoided by each of the associations. The belief prevails that limited memberships allow for more meaningful member participation. There is, nonetheless, excellent cooperation between the various associations. Although their constitutions differ in some respects, the common purpose of the regional associations is to sponsor such convention programs, workshops, and research as will help increase the professionalization of counseling and placement functions in student personnel work.

There are eight placement associations, each self-governing and independent, in the United States and Canada:

Eastern College Personnel Officers
Middle Atlantic Placement Association
Midwest College Placement Association
Rocky Mountain College Placement Association
Southern College Placement Association
Southwest Placement Association
University and College Placement Association (Canada)
Western College Placement Association

While the criteria for membership in each of the regional associations vary, each generally admits placement educators representing accredited, four-year, degree-granting colleges and universities, as well as employer representatives actively engaged in the recruitment of college graduates.

Eastern College Personnel Officers

ECPO, founded on October 15, 1926, antedated other regional placement associations by more than 20 years. The inspiration, planning, and launching of this first regional placement association is credited to a group of five dedicated visionaries: Paul W. Viets, supervisor of placement training at the Massachusetts Agricultural College, now the University of Massachusetts; Norman H. Abbott, director of placement at Boston University; Walker W. Daly, secretary for student employment at Harvard College; Raymond P. Miller, a member of the Division of Industrial Cooperation of Massachusetts Institute of Technology; and Wallace M. Ross, general secretary of the MIT Christian Association.

The stated objective of the founding fathers was to promote professional improvement for the members through an interchange of information on common problems. Over the years, this objective has been realized through a variety of activities—the annual convention, workshops for placement educators and for employer representatives, association-sponsored studies and research, the aiding of emerging colleges in the establishment of career counseling programs and offices. Because the founding fathers planned well, ECPO's precepts and organizational pattern served as a model for seven new associations that sprang into existence following World War II.

Rocky Mountain College Placement Association

Rocky Mountain has the reputation of being placement's second oldest regional association; it was organized in December 1947. R. Fred Chambers, director of placement at the University of Colorado, was the guiding force behind that new association. He was assisted by Herald L. Carlston, director of placement at the University of Utah; M. Helen Carpenter, then assistant director of placement at the University of Colorado; Jack Clevenger, dean of students, Lyle N. Slonecker, director of placement, and Mrs. S. Genevieve Fisher, assistant director of placement—all at Colorado State University; Bradford H. Prince, director of placement at the University of New Mexico; Richard T. Purcell, director of placement at the University of Denver; and Mrs. Goldie Slingerland, director of placement at New Mexico State University.

Southern College Placement Association

Under the leadership of Deans George C. Griffin and Fred W. Ajax at Georgia Institute of Technology, Southern College

Placement Association was organized on January 16, 1948. At the first business meeting, attended by 39 university and employer representatives, Dean Griffin was named president; Dean Earl C. Davis of Centre College of Kentucky, vice president; and Anne Seawell of the University of Georgia, secretary.

Middle Atlantic Placement Association

MAPA came into being on October 5, 1948 at the University of Delaware with a sizable group of placement officers involved: Col. D. M. Ashbridge, director of the Business Guidance and Placement Bureau, University of Delaware; Robert L. D. Davidson, director of placement, Temple University; Charles H. Ebert, Jr., director of placement at the University of Pittsburgh; Harold Fischer, professor of business administration at Franklin and Marshall College; George N. P. Leetch, placement director at Pennsylvania State University; E. Robins Morgan, placement director at Lehigh University; Fred W. Slantz, placement director at Lafayette College; E. Craig Sweeten, placement director at the University of Pennsylvania; and Charles E. Wangeman, placement director at Carnegie Institute of Technology.

One of the first objectives of MAPA was to develop a program of assistance to colleges that were initiating or expanding their placement services. One of the highlights of the year is the Gordon A. Hardwick Award which is presented by MAPA to the author of the best article of the year in the *Journal of College Placement*.

Midwest College Placement Association

MCPA, organized on June 7, 1949, quickly became the largest regional association with over 1,000 members. Its size, the diversity of its membership, which includes many employer representatives, as well as its strong leadership, has enabled

MCPA to sponsor several notable studies and research projects that have contributed considerably to present practices and knowledge.

The founding group of MCPA included Wendel W. Burton, employment director-salaried personnel, Minnesota Mining and Manufacturing Company; F. Lynn Cason, coordinator of placement, Purdue University; Harold S. Dawson, director of placement and associate dean of students, University of Illinois; Henry G. Goehring, placement director, College of Engineering, University of Wisconsin; Lawrence R. Hillyard, engineering, science, and humanities placement director, Iowa State University; John E. Steele, associate director, Bureau of Personnel Relations and Placement, Ohio State University.

Southwest Placement Association

SWPA was established on October 27, 1949. The guiding leadership was provided by George E. Bushong, alumni secretary and placement director at Southern Methodist University; Dr. Charles T. Clark, director, Student Employment Bureau, University of Texas; David Y. Robb, director of employment and placement, Southern Methodist University. The founding committee included Joseph Farrar, Ralph Frede, and Mrs. Helen Patterson, Office of Student Employment and Placement, University of Texas; Bertie Hammond, Texas Women's University; Wendell R. Horsley, director of placement services, Agricultural and Mechanical College of Texas; Frank A. Ives, director of Employment Service, University of Oklahoma; T. S. Richardson, dean of students, and E. M. Sowell, dean of the School of Business Administration, Texas Christian University.

Western College Placement Association

Mrs. Florence B. Watt, director of the Vocational Placement Bureau, University of Southern California, after an investigation of regional placement associations in the East, convened the first West Coast placement group on January 19, 1951, in Los Angeles. Assisting Mrs. Watt in the formation of WCPA were M. H. Allen, Prudential Insurance Company of America; Kenneth G. Beyer, Whittier College; Walter M. Bristol, Washington State University; Lucien Escallier, Loyola University; Mildred L. Foreman, director of the Bureau of Occupations, UCLA; R. E. Reynolds, Redlands College; Chase Sweetser, Coca-Cola Bottling Company; and William L. Wheaton, Pomona College.

In 1954 WCPA drew up a new constitution which, among other changes, opened membership "to any college in the western states granting baccalaureate degrees" and to "any employer who selects, trains, and places college graduates."

WCPA has been distinguished by the creation of the Vera Christie Graduate Fellowship which provides annual fellowships of $1,000 each for original research in the field of college recruitment and placement. The award is in the memory of Vera L. Christie, who was manager, Bureau of Occupations, University of California—Berkeley from 1928–1956. At the time of her death in 1956, she was president-elect of WCPA.

University and College Placement Association

The youngest of the placement associations is Canada's UCPA, formed on June 2, 1952. Over the years, it has made great strides and today it has flourishing programs in research, publications, and workshops. In early 1970, it obtained a new charter, established its own professional staff with a full-time executive director, and launched the Canadian equivalent of the *College Placement Annual*.

The charter group responsible for the formation of UCPA included John E. Andoff, McMaster University; J. Kenneth Bradford, University of Toronto; Thomas L. Hoskin, University of Western Ontario; W. Caron Jones, University of Toronto; John F. McLean, University of British Columbia; the

Rev. R. H. Shevenell, University of Ottawa; and David D. Smith, Sir George Williams College.

The College Placement Council

In 1957 the eight regional associations formed a national federation of placement associations, the College Placement Council. Since the regional associations are largely operated on a volunteer basis, the various services, so important to the work of their members, have been made the responsibility of the non-profit Council, which is headquartered in Bethlehem, Pennsylvania. Here the college placement and recruitment interests of more than 1,300 colleges and universities and of some 2,200 employers are implemented.

Memberships are not held in the Council but rather in one or more of the regional associations, which continue to be autonomous and self-governing. The Council consists of three elected representatives from each of the associations, an eight-member Board of Directors, with one member from each association, and six officers.

Initially, CPC was visualized as a clearing house for the associations and as a publishing organization for such periodicals and brochures as might serve the field. However, over the years the Council has become, increasingly, the center for communications and the source of information on college-trained manpower in the United States and Canada.

In the last few years, in particular, the CPC program has taken on new dimensions—in data processing, research, professional development, promotion of workshops, and vocational guidance materials.

With the creation of the CPC Foundation, a budding research program has begun to bear fruit. Early studies have covered student attitudes toward business careers as well as job expectations, satisfactions, mobility, and turnover among college graduates. Another important new adjunct is the CPC Research Information Center, which houses one of the largest collections of material pertaining to college-trained manpower. The Center has published the *Bibliography of Selected Research and Statistical Studies Pertaining to College-Trained Manpower, 1960–66,* as well as a supplement to the *Bibliography* which covers material received to April 1969.

The Council has also pioneered in computerized applications for the placement-recruitment field. A new approach to alumni service was opened with the GRAD System, a referral program which utilizes the computer to match college-trained candidates with suitable employment opportunities. Still other applications of the computer, as well as other forms of technology, are anticipated as placement and recruitment adopt new methods and techniques (see Chapter 8, Automation in Placement).

An early Council interest in assistance to traditionally Negro colleges has evolved into the formation of a separate non-profit corporation, College Placement Services, which shares facilities at the Council headquarters and is closely affiliated with CPC in its educational objectives. It is playing a major role in assisting underprivileged colleges to acquaint their students with expanding professional and vocational opportunities. Through corporation and foundation grants, it is fostering the establishment and implementation of various programs of assistance to these institutions, as described on later pages.

Publishing remains a major Council function, and the list of CPC printed material continues to grow.

The major publications are the *Journal of College Placement* and the *College Placement Annual.* The *Journal,* published four times during the college year, is considered the professional publication for the placement and recruitment field. The *Annual,* widely recognized as the most complete directory of occupational opportunities available to college graduates, is distributed, without charge, to graduating seniors and alumni through their college placement offices and to Armed Forces personnel around the world, through the United States Department of Defense.

Another nationally known publication is the Council's *Salary Survey,* which provides data on beginning salaries being offered currently on the bachelor's, master's, and doctoral-degree levels.

Still another important link in the Council's communications network is the newsletter, *Placement Perspective,* which reports on Council meetings and programs, regional association news of national interest, and special topics affecting the placement-recruitment field.

Other CPC publications include: *A Manual for Campus Recruiters,* a booklet providing guideposts for those engaged in employment of college graduates; *Preparing the Recruitment Brochure,* a checklist for those devising employer literature; *Placement Guides,* a similar checklist for the services of a placement office; *Directory of College Placement Offices,* an annual listing of placement offices and their directors; *Principles and Practices of College Placement and Recruitment,* a statement of ethical concepts for the student, the college, and the employer; *Organizing Workshops,* a manual designed to assist in the planning and staging of placement and recruitment workshops; *Philosophy of College Placement; Annotated Index of Journal Articles;* and standardized forms which can be adapted for use in individual placement and recruitment programs.

CPC has also called upon the medium of motion pictures. It has produced a 25-minute, color film "Where Do I Go From Here?" to portray the role college placement plays in helping to prepare students for sound career decisions. The film is now out of print, but new productions may be considered to depict the field of career counseling and placement in the Seventies.

Recognizing the need for improved counseling material, if a more adequate counseling job is to be done by the placement office, the Council most recently has established the CPC Career Information Advisory and Review Committee. A special review board studies new occupational literature as it is published and reports its findings regularly in the *Journal of College Placement.*

As the placement-recruitment profession continues to grow and mature, it is expected that the Council will be called upon by the regional associations to provide an even greater array of services.

College Placement Services

College Placement Services, Inc., established in 1965 as a non-profit, tax-exempt service and advisory corporation, has as its principal objective assisting the development and establishment of career counseling and placement offices at underprivileged educational institutions. Funded by grants from foundations, industry, and government, CPS has initiated and implemented various programs of assistance which have been directed to the traditionally Negro colleges.

These include: (1) sponsoring seminars and summer institutes for placement personnel from these colleges; (2) sending on request, advisory teams of specialists who submit recommendations to the administration of a college for the initiation or improvement of a career counseling and placement program; (3) acting as a cooperating agency in the submission of proposals to the United States Office of Education for financial grants under Title III of the Higher Education Act of 1965; (4) publishing and distributing guidelines for college placement activities particularly intended for developing educational institutions; (5) producing student motivational films and directing special student motivational programs; (6) developing fellowship and internship programs that provide academic training and work experience for graduate students seeking to enter the college placement field at traditionally Negro colleges.

CPS has used a variety of techniques in the training of placement personnel: on-the-job training at a college that has an established placement operation; sponsoring of individuals to attend workshops conducted by regional placement associations or ongoing academic programs at colleges and universities; and direct sponsorship and operation of institutes and workshops.

CPS advisory teams visited approximately 60 traditionally Negro colleges during the first three years of operation. Teams submit their findings in a report which is presented to the president of the college. An active follow-up campaign and other programs of assistance are then initiated so that the college will be able to implement or adapt as many of the team's recommendations as possible. These recommendations include a philosophical framework for college placement, as well as procedures, policies, and operations, organizational and staffing guidelines, plans and physical layouts of offices, budgets, equipment requirements, etc.

CPS has also served as a cooperating institution with developing colleges that were awarded grants for the improvement of placement programs under Title III of the Higher Education Act of 1965. The impact has been significant. In 1969, for example, 41 traditionally Negro colleges were awarded such grants in aid totaling $630,000.

The Sears Roebuck Foundation has provided financial support for a CPS-Duke University fellowship and internship program consisting of two years of formal graduate study and apprenticeship in vocational guidance and counseling at Duke University. Courses lead to a master's degree in guidance. Stipends provide tuition and living allowance for two graduate fellows. It is hoped that these students will then pursue careers in placement at the traditionally Negro colleges.

Through a special grant from the Ford Foundation in 1967, College Placement Services was able to produce, "Do They Really Want Me?," a 28-minute sound and color motion picture which documents the problems and opportunities facing black college graduates who seek careers in areas previously closed to them. In the first 14 months following its release, approximately nine million persons throughout the United States viewed the film.

Under a grant from the Ford Foundation, College Placement Services sponsored a New Career Opportunities program. The program was originated in 1968 under the sponsorship of the National Urban League, also with financial assistance from the Ford Foundation. The purpose of the New Career Opportunities program was to bring recent graduates who are employed in junior executive positions in business, industry, and government, back to their alma mater to meet with current students and faculty members in order to facilitate a direct exchange of information about the accessibility of new career fields for young black college graduates.

Forty-eight traditionally Negro colleges with an enrollment exceeding 100,000 students participated in the project during the spring 1969 semester alone. Over 300 recent graduates from the participating colleges returned to their campuses to serve as student career advisors.

Through the generosity of over 180 corporations and individuals, several hundred thousand dollars have been contributed to the CPS College Assistance Fund which has arranged grants to traditionally Negro colleges to further the development of their career counseling and placement programs.

How Does One Gain Membership in Regional Associations?

For the newcomer, it is not always easy to locate readily the officers and the membership secretaries of the regional associations. The College Placement Council, located in Bethlehem, Pennsylvania, can be of considerable help in supplying a variety of information to placement educators. Address your inquiries to:

> The College Placement Council, Inc.
> 65 East Elizabeth Avenue
> P.O. Box 2263
> Bethlehem, Pennsylvania   18001

Generally, membership in regional associations is restricted to active practitioners of college placement, counseling, and employer representatives. There are no educational or experiential requirements. In some regions employer membership is restricted by formula; in other associations the doors are wide open to employer members.

The American College Personnel Association

Another professional organization which can contribute both in general and specific ways to the placement educator is the American College Personnel Association. ACPA is the largest national professional organization for personnel workers in higher education. It has a four-fold purpose: (1) to promote the professional development of college student personnel workers; (2) to exercise leadership in identifying and resolving professional issues; (3) to stimulate research in student personnel work, and disseminate research findings; and (4) to recommend educational policies and legislation which implement the philosophy of student personnel work.

ACPA sponsors a variety of activities to accomplish its purposes: *The Journal of College Student Personnel;* the publication of monographs on a variety of student personnel subjects; appearance at Congressional hearings on legislation affecting higher education; the annual convention; and the work of the various commissions.

ACPA Commissions

The various issues and concerns of student personnel are pursued by the 14 commissions of ACPA:

1. Organization, Administration, and Development of Student Personnel Services
2. School-College Relations, Admissions, and Orientation
3. Student Residence Programs
4. Students, Their Activities, and Their Community
5. Financial Aid
6. Placement
7. Counseling
8. Student Health

9. Testing and Prediction of Academic Success
10. International Dimensions of Student Personnel Work
11. Student Personnel Programs in Junior Colleges
12. Professional Education of Student Personnel Workers in Higher Education
13. Student Personnel Work for Adults in Higher Education
14. Academic Affairs

The reader will note that a great variety of interest groups exist. Of special interest to the placement educator should be Commissions 4, 6, 7, and 9.

Membership in ACPA

Any person whose work responsibility includes student personnel work, such as teaching, administration, counseling, or research in higher education, is eligible for membership. For details write:

> APGA Association Services
> 1605 New Hampshire Avenue, N.W.
> Washington, D.C. 20009

Other Professional Organizations

ACPA is one of several divisions of the American Personnel and Guidance Association. Other divisions of APGA are:

The Association for Counselor Education and Supervision
National Vocational Guidance Association
Student Personnel Association for Teacher Education
American School Counselor Association
American Rehabilitation Counseling Association
Association for Measurement and Evaluation in Guidance
National Employment Counselors Association

Perhaps the reader's interest may be better served by one of the above divisions of APGA. Placement directors involved in educational placement will want to investigate Association for School, College, and University Staffing.

In addition to the various divisions of APGA, there are many other professional associations; however, none deals as directly with counseling and placement as those already described.

CHAPTER 15

The Outlook for Career Counseling and Placement

Placement Yesterday

THE DEPRESSION OF THE 1930s forced colleges to show concern for the job needs of their graduates. Many a placement office was born of this particular need to help a graduate find a job. World War II and the accompanying pressures of manpower needs in the national defense effort forced placement into a new service role: to help the employer find employees. With the population explosion following World War II, and the desire of the veteran-student to get on with life, there was need to serve two masters, the graduating student and the employer. In this dual role, the placement services of a college thus became expected and, as a consequence, widely accepted.

For a time some placement offices perceived their roles simply as bureaus of appointments where the employer and the student were brought together for a very simple purpose, the exchange of information. The student had the opportunity to tell a prospective employer about himself, and the employer had the opportunity to communicate information about his company with the hope that for many a student and company the result would be a happy job-marriage. Following World War II, when the traffic both in student job-hunters and employers became unbearably heavy, few placement directors found the time to do little more than direct the traffic.

Placement Today

There is a rather general consensus today that placement involves more in terms of service than arranging appointments and directing the traffic. It also implies counseling—counseling, at least in part, of a vocational nature. This is in addition to developing contacts with employers for full-time and part-time employment. Hence, the new designation over the placement office door: Office of Career Counseling and Placement.

But what is counseling of a vocational nature? Froehlich has said:

> "There is only one kind of counseling . . . Its objective is to assist individuals in making choices which will lead to lives which are individually satisfying and socially effective. Counseling is a process by which an individual is stimulated to: (1) evaluate himself and his opportunities; (2) make a feasible choice in the light of his unique characteristics and opportunities; (3) accept responsibility for his choice; and (4) initiate a course of action consonant with his choice." [1]

Froehlich distinguishes between counseling, teaching, and psychotherapy:

> "What is individual teaching? It is the process of providing learning experiences in line with a student's needs. Counseling differs from instruction in its basic assumption. Counseling assumes the foundation of experience and information upon

which choices can be made. On the other hand, in-
struction of individuals, either singly or in groups,
assumes that learning experiences are needed to
provide the foundation upon which choices can be
made . . . Counseling also differs from psychotherapy . . . the objective of psychotherapy is the
treatment of illness . . . Although many of the
techniques of teaching and psychotherapy are in-
terchangeable with those of counseling, the objectives are not . . ." [2]

Reflection upon the Froehlich point of view leads to the
understanding that the career counselor assumes each of these
roles, time and again, as he works with students.

A widespread point of view held by many college and university counseling departments is expressed by Gordin:

"Somehow I find it neither credible nor fruitful to
conceive of individuals as having vocational problems which are not at the same time personal problems or vice versa. I find it hard to recognize such
distinctions with our growing awareness of the
dynamic organizations of human attitudes and motives. I find it hard to reconcile these distinctions
with specific instances such as I encountered recently in talking to a student veteran about his
vocational plans. For two interviews we went
through a process familiar to those who think of
their job as vocational counseling. The student
took tests; we discussed test results and their significance for various vocational alternatives; we
discussed general information about the jobs involved. At the end of two interviews, we had reviewed all the surface aspects of the decision facing
him and were beginning to dig a little deeper into
the attitudes that might be the final determinants
of his vocational choice. No sooner had we started
on this process than our discussion took an entirely

new turn. In talking about some of his vocational motivations, he was directly led to expressions of some of his attitudes toward his life goal; and this in turn led him to discuss factors that had influenced these attitudes.

"The central factor, the one which was apparently placing the largest obstacle in the way of his clarity of vision, was the problem of his parents' adjustment to each other and his adjustment to them. His pent-up feelings came out in a flood. He poured out his hatred toward his mother and his desire to get away from her. Yet, he also identified with his father and felt the need to stand by him.

"We went on for four more hour-interviews exploring the ramifications of these feelings. He analyzed and re-analyzed his parents' relationship to each other and what position he could take on the matter. This problem had been puzzling him for a number of years. The directions he took in solving this difficulty would have an important influence on the direction he took with other problems. It involved such things as where he wanted to work, whether he wanted to get married, and whether he could ever have a feeling of security about himself. Eventually he came to a resolution of this central problem and turned once more to the question of vocational choice, this time dispatching it with decisiveness and reality." [3]

This illustration serves to point out that in Gordin's opinion, a point of view shared by many psychologists, choosing a job is more than simply job interviewing to find the right employer; it also illustrates the artificiality of fragmented counseling; i.e., educational counseling, personal counseling, vocational counseling. The example further demonstrates a clinical viewpoint, namely that both the problem of vocational choice and the personal adjustment problems were but parts of a total adjustment situation, and that the parts had to be related to the whole in order to affect a solution to any part of the problem.

Conflict Within Counseling Academe

Many career counselors and placement directors bristle at this clinical point of view. They argue, and quite justly, that they have been at it too long, and that they are too wise in experience, themselves, to agree that there is any one school of thought that holds the one right approach to counseling. Not a few students and placement personnel are aware of the inadequacy of much college vocational counseling today.

Here's what Robert Hoppock has to say about this inadequacy: "What we now have in vocational counseling is far too many psychologists who regard placement as a dirty word, and any direct contact with the employment market as degrading." [4]

From the foregoing there is the suggestion that there is not exactly unanimous agreement in counseling academe. In fact, on some campuses there is a considerable separation between the departments of counseling services and placement and substantial estrangement between counseling, placement, and faculty.

Every survey that the author knows which attempts to get at the relationship between counseling and placement uncovers a very tenuous connection between these two services. In a recent study of 67 major universities and colleges, Kirk [5] found that few counseling and placement services work together; that referrals by one service to the other are made only occasionally; that in many colleges these two departments are, in fact, in competition with one another in maintaining occupational libraries and in employment counseling. The author, as past chairman of Commission VI on Placement of the American College Personnel Association, has discovered that even at executive committee levels, where understanding and cooperation between counseling and placement might hope to be found, one, instead, finds placement workers looked upon as second-class citizens.

In a paper [6] presented at the Harvard Center for Careers, Robert Calvert, Jr. observed that "despite its tremendous progress in the past 20 years . . . a major problem has been the isolation of placement officers from their professional colleagues in guidance and from other administrators and faculty members on their own campuses." Among the reasons suggested by Calvert for this isolation is that "often the placement officer is appointed from a business background, and, therefore, does not readily identify with the guidance movement . . ." [6]

Some of the responsibility for lack of understanding and cooperation within the college student personnel family must be accepted by the student personnel workers themselves. On this point Williamson has said: "In the past some counselors have staked out their claims, erected barbed wire fences, electrified these wires, posted signs—'no trespassing by the faculty.' Such a practice is not only illegal, since the faculty has jurisdiction over the total educational program, but it also produces ignorance, neglect of personnel functions by teachers, irritation, resentment, and even active opposition." [7]

The faculty must also bear some responsibility for the alienation which exists between them and personnel services. Brunson has said:

> "Since the philosophies of faculty members of any institution of higher learning frequently range from the extreme rationalist approach on the one hand to the instrumentalist on the other, it is difficult in many situations to effect a meeting of minds on the importance or place of guidance in the total educational program. The rationalist, to whom cultivation of the intellect is the end of education, may regard guidance (hence placement) as 'overpaternalism' . . . The neo-humanist more readily acknowledges the fact that students have bodies, emotions, and feelings, but these he per-

ceives to be separated from the intellect . . . The instrumentalist, however, is satisfied only if he is involved in the total program of the college campus, for he regards the student as a dynamic Gestalt being educated by all the forces which the student meets in his day-by-day experience . . ."[8]

The problems produced by this dichotomous relationship between faculty and student personnel services, and within student personnel services between counseling and placement, can be attributed in some institutions to unrealistic institutional organization patterns and failure to give placement personnel faculty status. Perhaps, when placement workers show more serious concern about their own professional development, the establishment of minimum educational standards, and become concerned about entrance requirements to the profession, the respect of academe can be earned.

Placement Tomorrow

So, how do we close the gap between faculty and student personnel worker? Between counseling and placement? To begin with, the time is overdue for placement and counseling personnel to acknowledge that their lack of genuine concern about counseling philosophy has characterized the whole placement-guidance movement. It becomes necessary to understand, also, that this void in education has in itself engendered, in a large measure, a disrespect on the part of the faculty for student personnel workers in general. Action, now, to fill the void is essential.

Next, it might be acknowledged that heterogeneity, while colorful, is a serious drawback to professional development in placement. The diverse backgrounds of placement workers are often a barrier to communication and understanding and tend to promote a kind of provincialism in attitude. For example, the placement director with the engineering or music or business administration background may not, and often does not, understand the clinical approach to behavioral studies.

At the same time the wholly clinically oriented counselor who avoids the vocational aspects of counseling, whether he knows it or not, is often either talking or listening to himself; he just is not communicating either effectively or realistically with his student-client.

The various regional placement associations and the College Placement Council could give positive direction to professional growth by encouraging and stimulating dialogue on counseling philosophy. Leadership from the Council is needed in developing educational standards for and entrance qualifications to the profession. Failure on the part of the College Placement Council or the various regional placement associations to initiate professional standards will find, instead, professional standards being dictated by some other professional association.

In the present period of transition, what can be done to get placement workers to think more professionally? Some believe the College Placement Council, through the regional placement associations, has the responsibility to initiate, help fund, and help staff a series of continuing institutes and research to develop common learnings and understandings among the disciplines of psychology, counseling, and placement. Out of such beginnings could develop a body of professional knowledge compatible with modern research and thinking.

If the College Placement Council and the regional placement associations can manage such a project, the development of standards will not be an end in itself. The learnings and understandings that might become common could accumulate in a stockpile of intellectual raw material that would become communicable knowledge, thereby making the placement officer of greater service to education—which is what professionalization is really all about, anyway.

Professional growth is essential; it must be worked at not just because it will give status but because it will help placement workers do a better job of what they are doing. They must not get so bogged down in the day-to-day tasks of running an office that they shut themselves off from improving their competency as practitioners through participation in study, research, institutes, and forums with the long-term goal of professionalization.

In order to get a broad understanding of counseling and occupational adjustment, and thereby have background for the current dialogue in placement, the reader may wish to review such provocative writings as those of Frank Parsons, Anne Roe, Donald Super, and Carl Rogers. Parts I–IV of Williamson's "Trends in Student Personnel Work" [9] will be helpful in portraying the role of the counselor to date. To get the most critical analysis of vocational guidance yet made, the practitioner of vocational counseling will want to see himself as Barry and Wolf see him in "An Epitaph for Vocational Guidance." [10] It is the contention of these authors that most vocational counselors, consciously or unconsciously, operate within the framework of the Parsons hypothesis and that it is apathy on the part of placement personnel that has sustained the Parsons methodology (see Chapter 1). The authors believe that those practitioners who continue to adhere to the Parsons methodology "continue to operate on the basis of the myth that traditional methodological theory is applicable to the modern world." [11]

Barry and Wolf also contend that, because of blind adherence to the Parsons methodology, psychological testing becomes a standard procedure for many in career counseling:

> "Thanks to the methodological theory of Parsons which attempts to relate 'facts' about the individual to 'facts' about occupations to produce a reasoned occupational choice, testing is much in fashion in vocational guidance. Test scores have a spurious appearance of being 'facts' and yet they are not . . . Somehow in the process of trying to turn the students into a set of numbers, they, the counselors, lose sight of the essential humanity of the person behind the scores. Such a process ceases to be counseling and becomes judgment . . ." [12]

Epitaph for Vocational Guidance also attacks the so-called myth of factual information dispensed in career counseling. The authors imply that a reality is given to occupational information which is non-existent:

> "Basically the whole problem goes back to outmoded concepts of how students learn and make decisions. Regardless of wishful thinking and unrealistic theorizing, a vocational or educational decision is not an intellectual reasoning about two sets of questionable facts (Parsons' hypothesis). The 'facts' are unimportant unless they are dramatic and in conflict with the self-concept and firmly held values of the individual. The student makes decisions the way everyone makes them— out of the totality of his being." [13]

In most college placement offices, current theory and practice does suggest a Parsonian approach to vocational guidance. Hoppock rather succinctly states that "the basic problem in all vocational counseling is to help the client find out what he hopes to get from his job, what he has to offer in exchange for what he hopes to get, and in what occupations he will have the best chance of getting what he wants." [14] Even the classic definition of vocational guidance which was set forth by the National Vocational Guidance Association is Parsons inspired: "Vocational guidance is the process of assisting an individual to choose an occupation, prepare for it, enter upon it, and progress in it." [13]

There is good evidence that the majority of college placement offices do precisely what Hoppock suggests they do. Students are registered with the placement office. Talks by company representatives, alumni, and staff tell about the world of work. Occupational information libraries are maintained. Student interviews are held with counselors in order "to help the client find out what he hopes to get from his job, what he has to offer . . . and where he will have the best chance of getting what he wants." [15] Appraisals of students are prepared and company interviews arranged.

This or quite similar patterns of placement operation have persisted for half a century. It now becomes imperative that there be a re-examination of principles and practices in the light of new findings about individual behavior and development. Continuing present principles and policies just because they are widespread and have been followed for 50 years will be the surest way to obsolescence for placement and career counseling. There are those critics who predict career counseling will not survive because it cannot survive.[16] And it cannot survive, it is reasoned, because one cannot fragmentize individuals; people are whole persons, total personalities, and are to be counseled accordingly.

This holistic approach to individuals will, in time, erode the current principles and procedures of many a placement office. This approach to individuals merits the careful study of every career counselor, for the clinical evidence is impressive.

There is one thing certain about the future of placement—change. The old bureau of appointments, with the placement office serving primarily as a meeting place for employer and prospective employee, is gone forever. Placement tomorrow will need to articulate its basic educational mission—that of helping the student put together his jigsaw pieces of education and reason out his value orientations to life and the earning of a living. This mission, of course, implies counselor preparation essential to counseling the whole individual. It implies, too, a counseling philosophy rooted in sound, demonstrable principles of human behavior. This, in turn, means that much research must be forthcoming.

Sharp changes in procedures are just around the corner. For example, the cost of recruitment alone will force new and more effective ways of personnel selection, and the computer will play a major role in this process.

High on the list of priorities is the overcoming of student alienation and disaffection. Unless counselors have the intellectual capacity and flexibility to see the philosophic issues of our time through the eyes of the student, and work with him in solving the problems of the day, then counselors can be of little value.

There never was a greater need for problem-solvers in higher education. There never was a time of greater challenge for the placement educator.

BIBLIOGRAPHY

1 Farwell, Gail F. and Peters, Herman J., "Guidance Readings for Counselors," (Paper 45: Froehlich, Clifford P., *Counseling, Its Use and Abuse*), Rand Mc-Nally & Co., Chicago, 1961, pp. 370–371.

2 Ibid., p. 371.

3 Williamson, E. B., "Trends in Student Personnel Work," (A paper by Edward S. Gordin—"Counseling Point of View") pp. 120–121. University of Minn. Press, Minneapolis, 1949.

4 Hoppock, Robert, *Occupational Information*, McGraw-Hill, N. Y., 1963, p. 111.

5 Kirk, Barbara A., "Relations Between Counseling and Placement," *Journal of College Student Personnel, VI*, Sept., 1965, pp. 289 ff.

6 Calvert, Robert, Jr., "Placement and Career Counseling in a Large Coordinated University Program"—a paper presented at the Harvard Center for Careers.

7 Brunson, May A., *Guidance an Integrating Process in Higher Education*, Bureau of Publications, Teachers College, Columbia U., N. Y., 1959, p. 21.

8 Brunson, ibid., p. 18.

9 Williamson, ibid., pp. 1–135.

10 Barry, Ruth and Wolf, Beverly, *An Epitaph for Vocational Guidance*, Bureau of Publications, Teachers College, Columbia U., N. Y., 1962.

11 Ibid., p. 25.

12 Ibid., p. 56.

13 Ibid., p. 89.

14 Hoppock, Robert, *Occupational Information*, McGraw-Hill, N. Y., 1963, p. 149.

15 "The Principles and Practices of Educational and Vocational Guidance," *Occupations*, May, 1937, p. 772.

16 Barry, Ruth and Wolf, Beverly, op. cit., pp. 181 ff.

Glossary

Achievement test—This type of test attempts to measure how much a person has learned in a particular area: mathematics, English, etc.

Advising—The giving of information and advice. This is neither counseling nor guidance.

Aptitude—A predisposition to the learning of certain skills.

Aptitude tests—Tests which attempt to measure untrained potential skills: i.e., space relations ability, clerical aptitude, musical aptitude.

Aptitude surveys—Measures of feelings, ranging from birth control to politics. Most tests are neither reliable nor valid.

Capacity—Innate ability.

Career counseling—See counseling.

Character—The moral and ethical aspects of personality.

Coefficient of Correlation—A mathematical measure of the closeness of the relationship between two variables. A coefficient ranges from a maximum of $+1.00$ through zero to a maximum of -1.00.

Cognitive growth—Intellectual learning.

Computer time sharing—On-line computer time is shared by a variety of customers as a result of the volume capabilities of the computer. Service charges are contracted or figured at an hourly rate.

Continuum—Something that is absolutely continuous.

Counseling—A process by which the individual is stimulated to understand the totality of his personality—emotional, attitudinal, intellectual, and experiential—to the end that he may have a better understanding of the whole self and thereby respond effectively to the personal, educational, and vocational stimuli of his environment. Since the counselor is dealing with a total human being, counseling cannot, logically, be fragmented.

Developmental theory of choice—Vocational choice is a process rather than an event; choice is the consequence of developing interests, abilities, and personality traits over a considerable period of time.

Discontinuous growth—Growth is not steady; it is uneven; sometimes there are spurts; at other times, lags.

Ecology—That aspect of biology that deals with the relationships between organisms and their environment.

Exhibitionism—Behavior which attracts attention.

Guidance—An all-inclusive process of motivating the best development of the individual.

Heuristic theory—A theory, not yet proven, established for the purpose of stimulating research and investigation.

Interest inventory—A measure of an individual's likes and dislikes.

Occupational stereotyping—The evaluating of occupations on the basis of preconceived notions based on prejudice rather than on fact.

On-line computer service—Access to a computer through a computer terminal which is connected to the computer by telephone.

Personality—The individual as an entity, possessing qualities and traits that defy measurement and categorization.

Personality tests—Tests which attempt to describe and classify the individual's total behavior pattern. Most personality tests are neither reliable nor valid.

Placement—A means of helping students understand themselves through counseling, of aiding in the clarification of life goals and educational and job objectives through guidance, and of advising and helping to make employer contacts.

Psychoanalytic—Pertaining to Freudian psychology which emphasizes unconscious desires as motivators of behavior.

Psychological homeostasis—Bodily attempts to maintain psycho-logical equilibrium; the organism's attempt to create and maintain a compatible social environment in which the basic needs for love, security, approval, and prestige are satisfied.

Qualitative—A non-measurable quality or characteristic as compared to something which is measurable; i.e., character vs. weight.

Quantitative—Measurable mathematically.

Recruiter—An employer's representative whose responsibility is to seek out, interest, and identify potential employees.

Reliability—A test is statistically reliable if it is consistent with itself; that is, if on repeated testings it produces equivalent scores, which can be expressed in a positive statistical coefficient of correlation.

Role-play—The simulation of a particular behavior situation.

Self-concept—An individual's view of himself, his hopes, his aspirations, thoughts, feelings, values.

Sublimate—The indirect expression of a need, which cannot be satisfied directly, through some socially acceptable form of activity.

Validity—A test is valid if it actually measures what it was designed to measure and if this relationship can be expressed in a positive statistical coefficient.

Vocational Guidance—The process of helping an individual to understand himself and how work in a variety of forms implements and develops the self-concept.

Appendix

Many placement offices utilize this College Placement Council form, or an adaptation of it, to present information about students to employers.

2a	**CAMPUS RECRUITING INFORMATION FORM** (For submission by colleges to employers for data pertinent to setting up campus interviews.)	(COLLEGE NAME) Address

(USE SEPARATE FORM FOR EACH RECRUITING VISIT. Retain one copy for your file and return this form at least 4 weeks prior to interview date.)

EMPLOYER	ADDRESS	PHONE (Include Area Code)
NAME OF PERSON RESPONSIBLE FOR ARRANGEMENTS		TITLE

Types of Job Openings or Groups to be Interviewed*

	B.S.	M.S.	Ph.D.		B.S.	M.S.	Ph.D.
AERONAUTICAL ENGINEERING	—	—	—	CHEMISTRY	—	—	—
AGRICULTURAL ENGINEERING	—	—	—	GENERAL SCIENCE	—	—	—
ARCHITECTURE	—	—	—	GEOLOGY	—	—	—
ARCHITECTURAL ENGINEERING	—	—	—	INDUSTRIAL (BUS.) ADMINISTRATION	—	—	—
CERAMIC ENGINEERING	—	—	—	MATHEMATICS	—	—	—
CHEMICAL ENGINEERING	—	—	—	METALLURGY	—	—	—
CIVIL ENGINEERING	—	—	—	PHYSICS	—	—	—
ELECTRICAL ENGINEERING	—	—	—	STATISTICS	—	—	—
INDUSTRIAL ENGINEERING	—	—	—				
MECHANICAL ENGINEERING	—	—	—				
NUCLEAR ENGINEERING	—	—	—				
THEORETICAL & APPLIED MECHANICS	—	—	—				

DATE(S) OF INTERVIEWS	INTERVIEWS START AT	INTERVIEWS END AT: (Be sure of departure time before completing)

INTERVIEWING FOR THE FOLLOWING LOCATIONS

SCHEDULING INFORMATION*

Interview Information	NUMBER OF SEPARATE SCHEDULES WHICH SHOULD BE SET UP EACH DAY	LENGTH OF INTERVIEW (Indicate Choice) ☐ 20 Minutes ☐ 30 Minutes ☐ Other
Areas Of Employment And Training	☐ Design ☐ Research and Development	☐ Sales ☐ Sales Engineering ☐ Training Program
	☐ Accounting ☐ Finance	☐ Biochemistry ☐ Mechanical Engineering ☐ Other
Will Interview	☐ October Graduates ☐ January Graduates	☐ June Graduates ☐ Summer Graduates ☐ Other
Will Interview for Summer Work	☐ Freshmen ☐ Sophomores	☐ Juniors ☐ Seniors ☐ Graduate Students
Check (X) As Applicable	☐ Only recruiting visit to this office this school year	☐ Citizenship required ☐ Employer literature will be mailed 4 weeks prior to interview visit.

NAMES AND TITLES OF INTERVIEWERS

NOTE TO EMPLOYERS: For campus interviews, students use the College Interview Form CPC 1 as their resume.   DATE COMPLETED

CPC #2 — FORM ADOPTED BY THE COLLEGE PLACEMENT COUNCIL   *THESE ITEMS CAN BE ADJUSTED TO LOCAL SITUATIONS.

Placement offices can use this CPC form to gather information from employers regarding recruitment visits. Two other variants are available.

3 ⊕ **EMPLOYER INFORMATION SHEET** (For use by employers as a suggested format for submission of information to college placement offices.)	(EMPLOYER'S NAME) Address

NUMBER OF EMPLOYEES — DATE ESTABLISHED

LOCATIONS (Indicate Headquarters)

PRODUCTS OR SERVICES

POSITIONS FOR WHICH COLLEGE GRADUATES ARE NORMALLY EMPLOYED	ACADEMIC BACKGROUND DESIRED

METHOD OF TRAINING

OTHER INFORMATION

HOW TO APPLY FOR EMPLOYMENT

DATE

CFC #3 — FORMAT ADOPTED BY THE COLLEGE PLACEMENT COUNCIL

Employers can use this simple form to inform placement offices of positions for which they will be seeking candidates.

4 (GP) **COLLEGE INFORMATION SHEET**   (COLLEGE NAME)
       (For use by College Placement Offices as a suggested format for submission of information to employers.)   Address

ESTABLISHED ·   TYPE (Private, State, Community, etc.)

Placement Organization and Areas Serviced	_____Centralized _____Part-time _____Seniors
	_____Decentralized _____Summer _____Adv. Degree
	_____Coordinated _____Cooperative _____Alumni
	_____Other _____

Calendar and Grading Systems	_____Quarterly A = _____Points
	_____Semester **Dividing points for undergraduates:** _____Top Quartile _____3rd Quartile
	_____Trimester _____2nd Quartile _____4th Quartile

Dates to Avoid_____

Interview Period_____to_____each year.   Hours for Interviewing_____

How far in advance of date is schedule opened to students_____

Is pre-screening of resumes permitted?_____ If so, when?_____

Should employer call several days before interview visit? Yes_____ No_____

Material available to employer at time of campus interview:

Interviewing Information

_____ College Interview Form . . . ._____

_____Faculty Evaluations. . . . . . ._____   } Can employer keep these after the campus interview?

_____Transcripts . . . . ._____

_____Other. . . . . ._____

Arrangements for special contacts with students (e.g. group meetings, dinners, breakfasts)

Facilities

Parking Facilities_____
Location of Placement Office(s) and How to Reach (Where possible, attach map of campus with placement office(s) marked and travel directions with best modes of transportation)

Overnight Reservations_____

Enrollment

_____Day _____Night _____Undergraduate _____Graduate
Attach a tabulation showing the number of seniors and graduate students enrolled by major, by graduation date, and by degree.

PLACEMENT OFFICIAL   ADDRESS   PHONE

If several, please attach extra sheet(s)

NOTE: To be sent annually at least four weeks before recruiting season begins.   DATE COMPLETED

CPC #4 · FORMAT ADOPTED BY THE COLLEGE PLACEMENT COUNCIL

This college information sheet can be sent by placement offices to employers in advance of recruiting visits. Reproduction proofs of this and the other three forms can be obtained from the Council office.

CAMPUS INTERVIEWING SCHEDULE

COLLEGE _____

COMPANY _____

REPRESENTATIVE _____

INTERVIEWING DATE _____

IN THE 'CONSTRUCTIVE COMMENT' SECTION BELOW, PLEASE INCLUDE YOUR THOUGHTS ON THE STUDENT'S STRONG AND WEAK POINTS, PREPARATION FOR THE INTERVIEW AND ANY OTHER FACTORS WHICH INFLUENCE YOUR DECISION. THIS WILL HELP US IN COUNSELING THE STUDENT. YOUR COMMENTS WILL BE TREATED CONFIDENTIALLY.

| TIME | STUDENT'S NAME | DEGREE-MAJOR | GRAD. DATE | *INTERESTED? | | | CONSTRUCTIVE COMMENT |
				YES	NO	?	

*WAS THIS INTEREST (OR LACK OF INTEREST) CONVEYED TO THE STUDENT DURING THE INTERVIEW? IF NOT, HOW WILL YOU LET HIM KNOW AND BY WHAT APPROXIMATE DATE? PLEASE COMMENT.

_____ NEXT YEAR'S INTERVIEWING DATE _____

PLEASE PROVIDE PLACEMENT OFFICE WITH CARBON COPIES OF FOLLOW-UP CORRESPONDENCE WITH STUDENTS.

A form of this type can be utilized by placement offices to have recruiters record their impressions of students interviewed.

BABSON ALUMNI ASSOCIATION
ALUMNI QUESTIONNAIRE
(Please Print)

Your Alumni Office is compiling a 50th Anniversary edition of the Alumni Directory. It takes only a few moments to complete this questionnaire. May I ask you, please, to give us this few minutes of your time to help your college develop this new Directory.   Henry A. Kriebel, President

Name_____
           (First)   (Initial)   (Last)

Home Address_____
                  (Number)   (Street)

_____
    (City or Town)   (State)   (Zip)

Employer_____
              (Name)   (Number)   (Street)

_____
      (City)   (State)   (Zip)

Family Business?   ☐ Yes   ☐ No

Your Occupational Title_____ Date of Birth_____
                                                   Month   Day   Year

Year in which you assumed present occupational title_____

EDUCATIONAL HISTORY

Your secondary school_____
                         Name   Year of Graduation

Years attended Babson from_____to_____

Did you receive a BSBA?   ___Yes ___No
Did you receive an MBA?   ___Yes ___No
Did you receive a certificate?   ___Yes ___No
Are you a non-degree alumnus?   ___Yes ___No
What year do you wish to use as your class year?_____
If you attended other colleges, please give:

_____
Name of college   Field of study   Degree   Years attended

_____
Name of college   Field of study   Degree   Years attended

FAMILY INFORMATION

Wife's maiden name_____
                      First   Middle Initial   Last

Wife's college (if any)_____
                          Name of college   Year of Graduation

Children:_____
         Name   Age   Secondary School   College attended
                                                 (If Babson, indicate class)

Findings from alumni association questionnaires, such as the one reproduced on these two pages, can also be utilized by the placement counselor to advantage.

BABSON ACTIVITIES
(Please check appropriate items)

1. ___Alpha Delta Sigma	9. ___Bus. Econ Club	17. ___Sinai Club
2. ___Alpha Kappa Psi	10. ___Collegiate Club	18. ___Other (Specify)
3. ___Delta Sigma Pi	11. ___Circle K	19. _____
4. ___SAM	12. ___The B Club	20. _____
5. ___Blue Key	13. ___Theater Guild	21. _____
6. ___Beta Gamma	14. ___Inter. Rel. Club	22. _____
7. ___Finance Club	15. ___Epicurean Soc.	23. _____
8. ___Marketing Club	16. ___Newman Club	24. _____

VARSITY ATHLETICS

1. ___Basketball	4. ___Tennis	7. ___Swimming
2. ___Soccer	5. ___Sailing	8. ___Lacrosse
3. ___Hockey	6. ___Golf	

GENERAL INFORMATION

What honors have you received? (Honorary memberships, degrees, citations, Who's
Who, etc.)

_____

_____

To what professional societies, fraternal and political organizations, clubs,
and associations do you belong?_____

_____

_____

Major community offices, directorships held:_____

_____

_____

Publications (articles, books):_____

_____

Other information about yourself:_____

_____

ALUMNI FOLLOW-UP FORM

OFFICE OF CAREER COUNSELING
BABSON COLLEGE
BABSON PARK, MASSACHUSETTS 02157

Name _____ Class_____ Degree_____

Home Address_____
           Number   Street

_____
      City   State   Zip
The following questions refer to your principal employment:
   (List jobs in reverse chronological order. If more than 3, use back of page.)

Present Job Title_____

Name of Company (employer)_____

Your Business Address_____

Employer's Principal Products or Services_____

Date of Employment_____
                                  Approx. No.
Company Owned by You or Your Family: Yes?_____No?_____Employees_____

Annual Earnings (current)_____
        (Please give one figure which combines basic gross salary with
        bonuses, commissions, cost of living allowance, etc.)

Previous Job_____

Name of Company_____

Dates of Employment: From_____To_____
                                  Approx. No.
Company Owned by You or Your Family: Yes?_____No?_____Employees_____

Reason for Leaving_____

Previous Job_____

Name of Company_____

Dates of Employment: From_____To_____
                                  Approx. No.
Company Owned by You or Your Family: Yes?_____No?_____Employees_____

Reason for Leaving_____

Periodic alumni follow-up studies can provide invaluable information. On this and the next page is the form used by the author's college.

-2-

What was your Babson major?_____

What military service have you had?   (Check here if none_____)

Branch_____   Final Rank_____

Dates: From:_____   To:_____

Further Obligations:_____
_____

What formal study have you done since you were at Babson? (Please indicate diplomas, certificates, or degrees?)
_____
_____
_____

In what business or community "extracurricular" activities are you involved?
_____
_____
_____
_____

Please give below, or on the back of the sheet any news of yourself, your job, your family, or community activities which we may give to the Alumni Office.
_____
_____
_____
_____
_____
_____
_____
_____

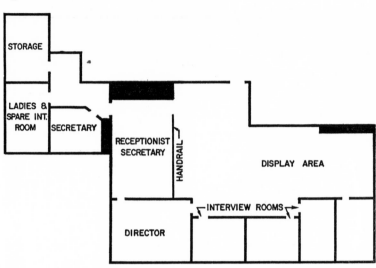

Here are the placement accommodations at two institutions with 3,000 to 4,000 enrollment. The plan at top utilizes relatively limited space effectively to serve the needs of a predominantly liberal arts student body. At the bottom is the arrangement for a placement office handling mostly students enrolled in technical curricula and requiring greater space because of the larger number of visiting recruiters.

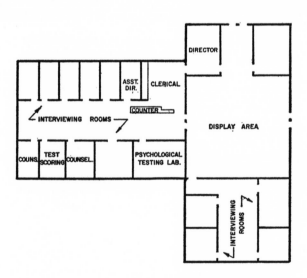

This is the floor plan for one of the country's newest and most complete place-ment offices (upper right). It was designed to have close proximity to other student services in the same building.

"Interview Guide"

Job Being Considered For:_____

Name:_____

Date:_____ Age:_____ Interviewer:_____

---

1. WORK HISTORY_____

                                                  Above avg.   Avg.   Below avg.

a. Duties
b. Likes
c. Achievements
d. Dislikes
e. Things done less well
f. Working conditions
g. Level of earnings
h. Reasons for changing jobs
i. Any leadership experience
j. Number of previous jobs
k. Factors of job satisfaction
l. Type of job desired
m. Total job accomplishment

---

2. EDUCATION AND TRAINING_____

                                                  Above avg.   Avg.   Below avg.

a. Best-poorest subjects
b. Grades
c. How much effort
d. Extra-curricular activities
e. Special achievements
f. Training beyond the undergraduate level
g. How was education financed
h. Total school achievement

---

3. EARLY HOME BACKGROUND_____

                                                  Above avg.   Avg.   Below avg.

a. Father's occupation
    (socio-economic level)
b. Temperament of parents
c. Number of brothers and sisters
d. How strictly raised
    (parental guidance)
e. Earliest age partially or wholly
    independent financially
f. Effects of early home influences

Reproduced on this and the next page is a guide developed by Richard A. Fear for a structured interview, as discussed in chapter 13, page 180.

-2-

4. PRESENT SOCIAL ADJUSTMENT_____
                                    Above avg.   Avg.   Below avg.

a. Present interests and hobbies
b. Marital status
c. Wife's interests and personality
d. Wife's attitude toward relocation
e. Attitude toward dependents
f. Financial stability
     (housing, insurance, etc.)
g. Health status
     (physical vigor and stamina)

5. PERSONALITY, MOTIVATION
   AND CHARACTER_____
                                    Above avg.   Avg.   Below avg.

   (+, A, -)

( ) a. Maturity   ( ) f. Tough-mindedness   ( ) k. Aggressiveness
( ) b. Emotional   ( ) g. Self-discipline   ( ) l. Conscientiousness
       stability,   ( ) h. Initiative   ( ) m. Hard worker
       even temper   ( ) i. Follow-through   ( ) n. Honesty and
( ) c. Teamworker   ( ) j. Self-confidence   sincerity
( ) d. Tact
( ) e. Adaptability

6. SUMMARY OF ASSETS   SUMMARY OF LIABILITIES

7. OVER-ALL SUMMARY

8. OVER-ALL RATING_____

     Excellent   Above average   Average   Below average   Poor

The Principles and Practices of
College Placement and Recruitment

GENERAL PRINCIPLES *

IT IS IN THE BEST INTEREST of students, colleges, and employers alike that the consideration of careers and selection of employment opportunities be based on an understanding of all the relevant facts and that these considerations be made in an atmosphere conducive to objective thought.

The recruiting of college students for employment by business, industry, government, and education should be carried out by the employers, candidates, and college authorities to serve best the following objectives:

1) The open and free selection of an employment opportunity that will provide the candidate with the optimum long-term utilization of his talents, consistent with his personal objectives.

2) The promotion of an intelligent and a responsible choice of a career by the candidate for his own greatest satisfaction and the most fruitful long-range investment of his talents for himself, for his employer, and for society.

3) The development of the placement function as an integral part of the educational system so that it, as well as the total recruiting process, may be oriented toward the establishment of high standards of integrity and conduct among all parties.

Employers recognize the desirability and necessity of effective communication and exchange of information with students,

---

*The General Principles section of this document was being updated by the College Placement Council at the time this section went to press.

faculty members, and college administrators. However, an employer should not be forced to meet with or to state his position to student groups as a condition of recruiting on campus.

PRINCIPLES

The Employer

1) Prior to, or at the time of the offer of employment, the employer should clearly explain to the candidate all conditions of employment.

2) The employer should give the candidate reasonable time to consider his offer, and in no case should the candidate be subjected to undue pressure to make a decision concerning employment.

3) The employer should not offer a candidate special payments, gifts, bonuses, or other inducements, nor should he compensate or favor a third party to prevail upon the candidate to accept an employment offer.

4) The employer should not raise salary offers already made, except when such action can be clearly justified as sound industrial relations practice, such as when an increase in hiring rate is required on an overall basis to reflect salary adjustments in the employing organization.

5) The employer should not ask the placement office to divulge salary offers made by other organizations or for confidential information of any nature.

6) The employer should avoid any arrangements that would provide preferential recruitment or extra assistance from any college by virtue of financial or other special considerations.

7) A. In recognition of the fact that the college placement function plays an integral role in the development of the student, *on-campus* recruitment activities should be conducted by the individual employer. Where unusual circumstances may require that the employer be represented by other than those directly responsible to man-

agement, such representation shall be in the name of the employer; and the employer shall assume full responsibility for any negotiations.

B.   The employer participating in recruiting activities related to graduating college students, but conducted *off-campus*, should take every reasonable precaution to assure that the sponsoring organization conducts its program in keeping with the spirit and intent of the Principles and Practices.

C.   The employer utilizing external recruiting media or programs directed toward those college students or graduates anticipating their first employment should assume reasonable responsibility for the reliability of representations made by such media or programs.

8)   When a candidate has declined an offer, the employer should accept that decision as final. If for any reason the employer wishes to re-establish contact with the candidate before graduation, he should do so only with a copy of his letter sent to the placement office.

9)   The employer should engage each candidate who has accepted his offer except when this becomes impossible because of (a) contingencies explained during the interview, or (b) unavoidable economic factors not foreseen when the offer was made.

COMPLIANCE

A complaint against an employer involving violation of these principles should be made in one of the following ways:

1)   Direct dialogue between the placement officer and employer concerned, or his superior; or

2)   A confidential report to the chairman of the ethics committee of the appropriate Regional Association for adjudication or hearing.

The Regional committee may refer the complaint to the College Placement Council's Principles and Practices Compliance

Committee for further interpretation or for information on past precedents, as required. Final adjudication, however, is the responsibility of the Regional Association involved.

SANCTIONS FOR VIOLATIONS

In cases referred to the Regional committees any necessary reprimand may take the form of:

1) A warning.
2) Suspension of privileges to attend an annual Regional meeting during a period of suspension determined by the Regional Association.
3) Forfeiture or denial of membership in the Regional Association.

The College

1) In counseling candidates, the placement officer and faculty members should not exert undue influence in the selection of positions.
2) The placement office constantly should be aware of its responsibility not to disclose any information given to it in confidence by employers or candidates as distinguished from information provided for general dissemination. Consequently, no employee of the placement office should divulge any salary information on a specific candidate to any employer.
3) The placement office may advise alumni that placement services are available if they are seeking a position. However, the placement officer should not contact an employed alumnus about a specific employment opportunity unless the alumnus has indicated that he is seeking a new position.
4) A college placement officer should avoid any arrangements that would provide preferential placement or extra assistance to organizations by virtue of financial or other special considerations.

5) In recognition of the fact that the college placement function plays an integral role in the development of the candidate, college placement officers and staff members should exercise restraint in the endorsement, or inferential endorsement, of proposed or existing placement and recruitment media. Such restraint shall be exercised especially until such time as the value of such media shall have been established by their contribution to student personnel services on the campus concerned.

COMPLIANCE

A complaint against a placement office involving violation of these principles may be made in one of the following ways:

1) Direct dialogue between the employer and the placement officer concerned, or his superior; or
2) A confidential report to the chairman of the ethics committee of the appropriate Regional Association for adjudication or hearing.

The Regional committee may refer the complaint to the College Placement Council's Principles and Practices Compliance Committee for further interpretation or for information on past precedents, as required. Final adjudication is the responsibility of the Regional Associations involved.

SANCTIONS FOR VIOLATIONS

In cases referred to the Regional committee, any necessary reprimand may take the form of:

1) A warning.
2) Suspension of privileges to attend an annual Regional meeting during a period of suspension determined by the Regional Association.
3) Forfeiture or denial of membership in the Regional Association.

PRACTICES AND PROCEDURES

The following are recommended operational procedures which are felt to serve the best interests of the employer, the college, and the candidate—as differentiated from the principles set forth in the preceding section.

The Employer

1) The employer should inform the placement office well in advance regarding desired interview dates, broad categories of employment expected to be available, college degrees, and other pertinent requirements. He should promptly advise the placement office of any change in his original request or subsequent arrangements.

2) The employer should provide suitable material to give students a true and factual picture of the employing organization. This material should be supplied in sufficient quantities and well in advance of the interviewing date.

3) When both the parent organization and subsidiary or affiliated organization conduct interviews in the same college, an explanation of their missions and exact affiliation should be made, both to the placement office and to the candidates.

4) The employer should be punctual. He should advise the placement office about his anticipated arrival and departure times. Every effort should be made to avoid last-minute cancellations.

5) The employer should follow the interview time schedule agreed upon with the placement office.

6) As soon as possible following an interview, the employer should communicate with the candidate and the placement office concerning the outcome of the interview.

7) If the employer invites a candidate to visit his premises

for further discussion of employment, the trip should be arranged to interfere as little as possible with class schedules. The employer should explain what expenses will be paid, how, and when. Invitations for this purpose should be made only on an individual basis and the employer should avoid elaborate entertaining or overselling.

8) No more than two and preferably only one interviewer should conduct an interview. The total number of interviewers brought on campus by an employer should not exceed the number necessary to handle adequately the number of candidates scheduled for interviews.

9) Arrangements for interview space requirements should be made in advance with the placement office.

10) Representatives of an employer, including alumni of the college, should notify the placement office of the college, in advance, of any plans for campus visits to acquaint faculty members or candidates with employment activities or opportunities. Such representatives should exercise scrupulous care to avoid undue demands on the time of faculty members or candidates.

11) An employer who desires to meet with a particular candidate at the time of his interview visit should communicate with the candidate well in advance with a notice to the placement office.

12) The employer should keep the placement office informed concerning his interest in particular candidates and his negotiations with them.

13) The employer should make certain that its representatives using placement office facilities are acquainted with this statement of "Principles and Practices of College Placement and Recruitment."

The College

1) The college should provide competent counseling service and such other assistance that will aid the candidate

in reaching a career decision based on a full appreciation of his potential.

2) As soon as the information is available, the placement office should inform employers about graduation dates and the number of individuals who are candidates for degrees in the various curricula of the college.

3) The placement office should make employment material available to candidates and faculty.

4) The placement office should not restrict the number of interviews per candidate, except as necessary to discourage indiscriminate "shopping."

5) The college should provide adequate space and facilities for quiet and private interviews.

6) Candidate resumes and/or related material should not be released to organizations other than to bona fide employers, and then only with the written permission of the candidate.

7) The placement office should arrange for employers to meet faculty members who know candidates personally and can provide information about their work and qualifications.

8) Alumni may establish files with the placement office at an institution other than their own, provided this arrangement is in keeping with the receiving institution's policy. They will be asked to furnish, for the cooperating institution's files, a statement from the placement officer of the college where they completed their studies.

9) The placement office should make certain that candidates using its facilities are acquainted with this statement.

10) As early as practicable, the placement office should announce the names of employers and the dates on which they will be recruiting on campus. Announcements should be made later to incorporate subsequent changes.

11) The placement office should inform candidates of the types of positions for which the employer will be interviewing on the proposed campus visit. To the extent of the time allotted for the campus visit, the placement

office should schedule appointments for interested candidates who appear to be qualified.

12) The placement office should inform employers planning to visit the campus about the response of the candidates. This will give the employer an opportunity to adjust the number of interviewers in accordance with the appointments scheduled.

The Candidate

1) In preparation for interviews with prospective employers, the candidate should analyze his interests and abilities, consider his career objectives, seek information about the fields of his interest through published materials and counseling, and organize his thoughts so that he may ask and answer questions intelligently.

2) The candidate should notify the placement office as early as possible of the interviews he wishes to have. He should also notify the placement office immediately if he subsequently finds that there is reason for him to cancel any appointments.

3) Before taking an interview, the candidate should read the company material and fill out such forms as may be required. He should arrive on time for his appointment and conduct himself in a businesslike manner.

4) The candidate who is invited to visit an employer's premises should promptly acknowledge the invitation and should accept only if he is sincerely interested in a position with that employer. If the candidate is to set the date of his visit, he should write the employer sufficiently in advance to permit the employer to confirm the date.

5) A candidate making a visit at an employer's expense should seek reimbursement only for those expenditures which pertain to the trip. If he visits other employers on the same trip, he should prorate the total cost among them.

6) When he receives an offer of employment, the candidate

should notify the employer as soon as possible, but no later than the deadline specified by the employer, whether he will or will not accept.

7) If a candidate has a legitimate reason for the extended consideration of more than one offer, he should not only notify employers whose offers he is refusing, but also communicate with employers under consideration to attempt to establish a mutually satisfactory decision date. He should make his final choice at the earliest possible date.

8) A candidate should realize that an employment offer is to be accepted in good faith and with sincere intentions of honoring the commitment. He should not thereafter present himself for interviews with other employers.

9) Throughout his negotiations for employment, the candidate should keep the placement office advised of his decisions.

COMPLIANCE

A complaint against a candidate involving a breach of ethical conduct in these matters should be made directly to the placement officer concerned. Sanctions, if required, should be as prescribed by that candidate's college or university. The placement officer should advise the employer registering the complaint of the disposition of the case.

Statement of the
Rights and Freedoms
of Students

(Drafted by representatives of the American Association of University Professors, U.S. National Student Association, Association of American Colleges, National Association of Student Personnel Administrators, and National Association of Women Deans and Counselors)

Preamble

Aᴄᴀᴅᴇᴍɪᴄ ɪɴꜱᴛɪᴛᴜᴛɪᴏɴꜱ ᴇxɪꜱᴛ for the transmission of knowledge, the pursuit of truth, the development of students, and the general well being of society. Free inquiry and free expression are indispensible to the attainment of these goals. As members of the academic community, students should be encouraged to develop the capacity for critical judgment and to engage in a sustained and independent search for truth. Institutional procedures for achieving these purposes may vary from campus to campus, but the minimal standards of academic freedom of students outlined below are essential to any community of scholars.

Freedom to teach and freedom to learn are inseparable facets of academic freedom. The freedom to learn depends upon appropriate opportunities and conditions in the classroom, on the campus, and in the larger community. Students should exercise their freedom with responsibility.

The responsibility to secure and respect general conditions conducive to the freedom to learn is shared by all members of the academic community. Each college and university has a duty to develop policies and procedures which provide and safeguard this freedom. Such policies and procedures should be developed at each institution within the framework of general standards and of the members of the academic community. The purpose of this statement is to enumerate the essential provisions for student freedom to learn.

I. Freedom of Access to Higher Education

The admission policies of each college and university are a matter of institutional choice provided that each college and university makes clear the characteristics and expectations of students which it considers relevant to success in the institution's program. While church-related institutions may give admission preference to students of their own persuasions, such a preference to students should be clearly and publicly stated. Under no circumstances should a student be barred from admission to a particular institution on the basis of race. Thus, within the limits of its facilities, each college and university should be open to all students who are qualified according to its admission standards. The facilities and services of a college should be open to all of its enrolled students, and institutions should use their influence to secure equal access for all students to public facilities in the local community.

II. In the Classroom

The professor in the classroom and in conference should encourage free discussion, inquiry, and expression. Student performance should be evaluated solely on an academic basis, not on opinions or conduct in matters unrelated to academic standards.

A. *Protection of Freedom of Expression.* Students should be free to take reasoned exception to the data or views offered in any course of study and to reserve judgment about matters of opinion, but they are responsible for learning the content of any course of study for which they are enrolled.

B. *Protection Against Improper Academic Evaluation.* Students should have protection through orderly procedures against prejudiced or capricious academic evaluation. At the same time, they are responsible for maintaining standards of academic performance established for each course in which they are enrolled.

C. *Protection Against Improper Disclosure.* Information about student views, beliefs, and political associations which professors acquire in the course of their work as instructors, advisers, and counselors should be considered confidential. Protection against improper disclosure is a serious professional obligation. Judgments of ability and character may be provided under appropriate circumstances, normally with the knowledge or consent of the student.

III. Student Records

Institutions should have a carefully considered policy as to the information which should be part of a student's permanent educational record and as to the conditions of its disclosure. To minimize the risk of improper disclosure, academic and disciplinary records should be separate, and the conditions of access to each should be set forth in an explicit policy statement. Transcripts of academic records should contain only information about academic status. Information from disciplinary or counseling files should not be available to unauthorized persons on campus, or to any person off campus without the express consent of the student involved except under legal compulsion or in cases where the safety of persons or property is involved. No records should be kept which reflect the political activities or beliefs of students. Provisions should also be made for periodic routine destruction of noncurrent disciplinary records. Administrative staff and faculty members should respect confidential information about students which they acquire in the course of their work.

IV. Student Affairs

In student affairs, certain standards must be maintained if the freedom of students is to be preserved.

A. *Freedom of Association.* Students bring to the campus a variety of interests previously acquired and develop many new interests as members of the academic community. They should be free to organize and join associations to promote their common interests.

1. The membership, policies, and actions of a student organization usually will be determined by vote of only those persons who hold bona fide membership in the college or university community.

2. Affiliation with an extramural organization should not of itself disqualify a student organization from institutional recognition.

3. If campus advisers are required, each organization should be free to choose its own adviser, and institutional recognition should not be withheld or withdrawn solely because of the inability of a student organization to secure an adviser. Campus advisers may advise organizations in the exercise of responsibility, but they should not have the authority to control the policy of such organizations.

4. Student organizations may be required to submit a statement of purpose, criteria for membership, rules of procedures, and a current list of officers. They should not be required to submit a membership list as a condition of institional recognition.

5. Campus organizations, including those affiliated with an extramural organization, should be open to all students without respect to race, creed, or national origin, except for religious qualifications which may be required by organizations whose aims are primarily sectarian.

B. *Freedom of Inquiry and Expression.*

1. Students and student organizations should be free to examine and to discuss all questions of interest to them, and to express opinions publicly and privately. They should always be free to support causes by orderly means which do not disrupt the regular and essential operation of the institution. At the same time, it should be made clear to the academic and the larger community that in public expressions or demonstrations students or student organizations speak only for themselves.

2. Students should be allowed to invite and to hear any person of their own choosing. Those routine procedures required by an institution before a guest speaker is invited to appear on campus should be designed only to insure orderly scheduling of facilities and adequate preparation for the event, and that the occasion is conducted in a manner appropriate to an academic community. The institutional control of campus facilities should not be used as a device of censorship. It should be made clear to the academic and larger community that sponsorship of guest speakers does not necessarily imply approval or endorsement of the views expressed, either by the sponsoring group or the institution.

C. *Student Participation in Institutional Government.* As constituents of the academic community, students should be free, individually and collectively, to express their views on issues or institutional policy and on matters of general interest to the student body. The student body should have clearly defined means to participate in the formulation and application of institutional policy affecting academic and student affairs. The role of the student government and both its general and specific responsibilities should be made explicit, and the actions of the student government within the areas of its jurisdiction should be reviewed only through orderly and prescribed procedures.

D. *Student Publications.* Student publications and the student press are a valuable aid in establishing and maintaining an atmosphere of free and responsible discussion and in bringing student concerns to the attention of the faculty and the institutional authorities and in formulating student opinion on various issues on the campus and in the world at large.

Whenever possible the student newspaper should be an independent corporation financially and legally separate from the university. Where financial and legal autonomy is not possible, the institution, as the publisher of student publications, may have to bear the legal responsibility for the content of the publications. In the delegation of editorial responsibility to students the institution must provide sufficient editorial freedom and financial autonomy for the student publications to maintain their integrity of purpose as vehicles for free inquiry and free expression in an academic community.

Institutional authorities, in consultation with students and faculty, have a responsibility to provide written clarification of the role of the student publications, the standards to be used in their evaluation, and the limitations on external control of their operation. At the same time, the editorial freedom of student editors and managers entails corollary responsibilities to be governed by the canons of responsible journalism, such as the avoidance of libel, indecency, undocumented allegations, attack on personal integrity, and the techniques of harassment and innuendo. As safeguards for the editorial freedom of student publications the following provisions are necessary:

1. The student press should be free of censorship and advance approval of copy, and its editor and managers should be free to develop their own editorial policies and news coverage.

2. Editors and managers of student publications should be protected from arbitrary suspension and removal because of student, faculty, administrative, or public disapproval of editorial policy or content. Only for proper and stated causes should editors and managers be subject to removal and then by orderly and prescribed procedures. The agency responsible for the appointment of editors and managers should be the agency responsible for their removal.

3. All university published and financed student publications should explicitly state on the editorial page that the opinions there expressed are not necessarily those of the college, university, or student body.

V. Off-Campus Freedom of Students

A. *Exercise of Rights of Citizenship.* College and university students are both citizens and members of the academic community. As citizens, students should enjoy the same freedom of speech, peaceful assembly, and right of petition that other citizens enjoy and, as members of the academic community, they are subject to the obligations which accrue to them by virtue of this membership. Faculty members and administrative officials should insure that institutional powers are not employed to inhibit such intellectual and personal development of students as is often promoted by their exercise of rights of citizenship both on and off campus.

B. *Institutional Authority and Civil Penalties.* Activities of students may upon occasion result in violation of law. In such cases, institutional officials should be prepared to apprise students of sources of legal counsel and may offer other assistance. Students who violate the law may incur penalties prescribed by civil authorities, but institutional authority should never be used merely to duplicate the function of general laws. Only where the institution's interests as an academic community are distinct and clearly involved should the special authority of the institution be asserted. The student who incidentally violates institutional regulations in the course of his off-campus activity, such as those relating to class attendance, should be subject to no greater penalty than would normally be imposed. Institutional action should be independent of community pressure.

VI. Procedural Standards in Disciplinary Proceedings

In developing responsible student conduct, disciplinary proceedings play a role substantially secondary to example, counseling, guidance, and admonition. At the same time, educational institutions have a duty and the corollary disciplinary powers to protect their educational purpose through the setting of standards of scholarship and conduct for the students who attend them and through the regulation of the use of institutional facilities. In the exceptional circumstances when the preferred means fail to resolve problems of student conduct, proper procedural safeguards should be observed to protect the student from the unfair imposition of serious penalties.

The administration of discipline should guarantee procedural fairness to an accused student. Practices in disciplinary cases may vary in formality with the gravity of the offense and the sanctions which may be applied. They should also take into account the presence or absence of an Honor Code, and the degree to which the institutional officials have direct acquaintance with student life, in general, and with the involved student and the circumstances of the case in particular. The jurisdiction of faculty or student judicial bodies, the disciplinary responsibilities of institutional officials, and the regular disciplinary procedures, including the student's right to appeal a decision, should be clearly formulated and communicated in advance. Minor penalties may be assessed informally under prescribed procedures.

In all situations, procedural fair play requires that the student be informed of the nature of the charges against him, that he be given a fair opportunity to refute them, that the institution not be arbitrary in its actions, and that there be provisions for appeal of a decision. The following are recommended as proper safeguards in such proceedings when there are no Honor Codes offering comparable guarantees.

A. *Standards of Conduct Expected of Students.* The institution has an obligation to clarify those standards of behavior which it considers essential to its educational mission and its community life. These general behavioral expectations and the resultant specific regulations should represent a reasonable regulation of student conduct, but the student should be as free as possible from imposed limitations that have no direct relevance to his education. Offenses should be as clearly defined as possible and interpreted in a manner consistent with the aforementioned principles of relevancy and reasonableness. Disciplinary proceedings should be instituted only for violations of standards of conduct formulated with significant student participation and published in advance through such means as a student handbook or a generally available body of institutional regulations.

B. *Investigation of Student Conduct.*

1. Except under extreme emergency circumstances, premises occupied by students and the personal possessions of students should not be searched unless appropriate authorization has been obtained. For premises such as residence halls controlled by the institution, an appropriate and responsible authority

should be designated to whom application should be made before a search is conducted. The application should specify the reasons for the search and the objects or information sought. The student should be present, if possible, during the search. For premises not controlled by the institution, the ordinary requirements for lawful search should be followed.

2. Students detected or arrested in the course of serious violations of institutional regulations, or infractions of ordinary law, should be informed of their rights. No form of harassment should be used by institutional representatives to coerce admissions of guilt or information about conduct of other suspected persons.

C. *Status of Student Pending Final Action.* Pending action on the charges, the status of a student should not be altered, or his right to be present on the campus and to attend classes suspended, except for reasons relating to his physical or emotional safety and well-being, or for reasons relating to the safety and well-being of students, faculty, or university property.

D. *Hearing Committee Procedures.* When the misconduct may result in serious penalties and if the student questions the fairness of disciplinary action taken against him, he should be granted, on request, the privilege of a hearing before a regularly constituted hearing committee. The following suggested hearing committee procedures satisfy the requirements of "procedural due process" in situations requiring a high degree of formality:

1. The Hearing Committee should include faculty members or students, or, if regularly included or requested by the accused, both faculty and student members. No member of the hearing committee who is otherwise interested in the particular case should sit in judgment during the proceedings.

2. The student should be informed, in writing, of the reasons for the proposed disciplinary action with sufficient particularity, and in sufficient time, to insure opportunity to prepare for the hearing.

3. The student appearing before the Hearing Committee should have the right to be assisted in his defense by an adviser of his choice.

4. The burden of proof should rest upon the officials bringing the charge.

5. The student should be given an opportunity to testify and to present evidence and witnesses. He should have an opportunity to hear and question adverse witnesses. In no case should the committee consider statements against him unless he has been advised of their content and of the names of those who made them, and unless he has given an opportunity to rebut unfavorable inferences which might otherwise be drawn.

6. All matters upon which the decision may be based must be introduced into evidence at the proceeding before the Hearing Committee. The decision should be based solely upon such matter. Improperly acquired evidence should not be admitted.

7. In the absence of a transcript, there should be both a digest and a verbatim record, such as a tape recording, of the hearing.

8. The decision of the Hearing Committee should be final, subject only to the student's right of appeal to the president or ultimately to the governing board of the institution.

Index